999 Ways 2 Say No 2 A "No-Good Man"

999 Ways 2 Say No
2 A "No-Good
Man"

Mercedes A. Terzol

iUniverse, Inc.
New York Lincoln Shanghai

999 Ways 2 Say No 2 A "No-Good Man"

iUniverse books may be ordered through booksellers or by contacting:

iUniverse
2021 Pine Lake Road, Suite 100
Lincoln, NE 68512
www.iuniverse.com
1-800-Authors (1-800-288-4677)

ISBN-13: 978-0-595-36760-3 (pbk)
ISBN-13: 978-0-595-81179-3 (ebk)
ISBN-10: 0-595-36760-7 (pbk)
ISBN-10: 0-595-81179-5 (ebk)

Printed in the United States of America

Contents

1

Introductory Remarks

Dedication:

This book is dedicated to womanhood. These words speak directly to the heart, soul, and spirit of every woman whose feet grace this earth. To the women who have ignited their own strength and who continue to learn how to apply courage to all endeavors of life, this book is especially dedicated to you. To the countless number of women who fight to ignite their dormant strength and to those who have not yet realized their strength, these words speak to you. Others may not always be present to provide those words of encouragement, but this book will.

Acknowledgments:

I would like to thank the Terzol family, especially my aunt, Augusta, and grandmother, Dorothy, for their years of love and dedication. To the Adams family, especially my aunt, Christina, and sister, Norma, thank you for your support. To a special friend, Shonté, I appreciate the good times. To Ruth and the Macklin family, especially Thelma, thank you for your words of encouragement. To those whom I did not mention, I offer my apologies. My love is undying for you all. Peace and blessings.

2

In the Name of Love: My Personal Testimony

It was the summer of 2003. The time approached three o'clock in the morning on a Thursday. On that night, my heart would not allow my eyes to rest. I tried to distract myself. I turned on the television set. Then I tried listening to some music. Nothing was successful. There was a reason for this. I had a strong desire to release what was within me. This had been brewing for quite some time, and I could not contain it any longer. Now I was aware of what I was about to do. I knew I was about to enter into the land of no return, the land where hearts are broken, the land where devastation lurks and claims so many victims. Was I fully prepared for the aftermath my mouth might bring to my heart if I shared my feelings? Yes. There is no doubt I was a little hesitant, but I still felt the need to proceed.

It was not until I picked up my telephone to dial the number that nervousness really crept into my body. My palms began sweating. My heart started racing. I dialed the number once, but I pressed the end button before the phone rang. After taking some time to get myself together, I picked up the phone and dialed the number again. It rang about five times.

I braced myself, crossed my fingers, and said, "I don't know how to tell you this," I paused, then confessed, "I love you."

I usually do not feel this type of emotion, let alone express it, but for once I managed to build up enough courage to release some of the control that I desire to have over my emotions and any given situation. After fifteen seconds of hearing his voice, I responded with my words after the beep.

The man whom I had fallen in love with was a sweet and calm soul. Intelligent and ambitious were also two adjectives applicable to him. He was not afraid to put his mind to use and think. His first love was writing, making a pen his favorite companion. Writing encompassed everything in his life. He had aspirations for his writing and worked hard to make them a reality. In fact, it was a combination of these qualities that would soon lead him to embracing music as his secondary path, aside from computer programming. From being a sketch artist to a musician, he truly was an inspired artist at heart. Initially, the amount of creativity that lingered beneath his surface was unknown to me. But that would soon change.

It was not until some time after I had expressed my feelings to him that I would discover he had recorded an album and managed to get signed to a record label. I was not surprised at this because I always knew he would do something wonderful with his life. In January 2004, his Web site, containing twenty songs, was put online for listeners to access. I truly did not realize just how talented and down-to-earth he actually was until I heard them. His style was smooth. His songs were powerful. The themes were varied. He was truly versatile.

Anxiously I waited and waited. But two weeks went by from that day in July, and there was still no response. I should have realized he didn't share my feelings when he did not respond to my phone call in a timely fashion. But like the fool for love I was, I tried to rationalize this and justify his not calling.

"Oh, he's out of town. That's why he can't get back to me. I know he feels the same way because he's still in contact with me after being separated for a long period of time. He's just afraid to confront his feelings," I assured myself.

As I continued to wait for his response, I made all of the excuses in the world on his behalf.

"He has had such a hard life, growing up in the midst of poverty, having sickle-cell anemia, experiencing those painful crises, hanging out with the wrong crowd, being exposed to violence, drugs, and the many other negativities that surround one in such an environment. It is not his fault. He'll eventually come around."

That is what I said to myself. I also asked myself, "Why, oh why am I so inclined to make excuses for this man?"

It was a way to ease the pain and continue my tolerance, for my heart would not permit me to acknowledge and accept the truth. I was in a vulnerable state. My heart, my love, everything was on the line. If I cut ties with him, I felt as though I would also be cutting the very veins that transported blood to my heart. Doing this would devastate me.

The primary reason I so willingly made excuses for him was because I had never before experienced a man who I felt was my other half or soul mate. Before meeting him, I never acknowledged the term itself, soul mate. I thought it was some type of hoax. I dismissed it as a way to convince the public not to relinquish the hope of one day finding a compatible mate. I laughed at the concept of there being one person who an individual is destined to be with and is also a perfect match. It was impossible for there to be one person who would go perfectly with me, I thought. But with him there was a deep affinity. Somehow he made my heart feel. My mind, therefore, understood the true meaning of love.

There was a common trend with me and relationships. In my experience with the opposite sex, I always encountered great difficulty in finding someone whom I could connect with on a mental level. Besides, I was always considered a very difficult person to relate to. I had certain standards that had to be met in order for the relationship to proceed to the next level. I believed that the only thing being too easy would deliver is quite a number of footprints etched across the backside.

I thought long and hard about the ingredients that make for a long-lasting and strong relationship. Of course physical attraction is important, but having a mental connection is just as important. Honesty, fidelity, commitment, and the stability of both partners are also important qualities. The idea of physical attraction would always remain the easy part of establishing an interest, but physical attraction alone was never enough to keep my interest. In general terms, physical appearance does not constitute the primary element in establishing a long-lasting relationship. If physical attraction is the primary element, the relationship will not evolve into something more serious and concrete.

It was during this time that reminiscing became my favorite pastime. I could remember the first time our eyes met. It was the first day of classes on September 4, 2000. The time was about three o'clock in the afternoon. I was coming from the college post office with my two roommates, and he was going to the post office with a friend of his. As they made a left turn, we made a right turn and his six-foot-two-inch, brown-toned body came into contact with mine at the window of the hallway. Our eyes crossed paths, and we stared at one another for about three seconds as our feet continued to move. His big brown eyes were so magnetic. He had an appealing innocence but with an intensity to it. From that stare, I sensed something special. I could feel it. Around 10 PM that night, I received a call from him. He introduced himself and told me of his future plans. He did not tell me everything there was to know, so there was still that feeling of intrigue. By the end of the conversation, it was about 11:30 PM. Somehow the time just seemed to fly by.

"Have a good night, Benz," were his parting words.

For the next two months of our relationship, we spent a considerable amount of time together. In between his hectic senior schedule and my adjustment to college life, we still managed to fit in time for each other. He was sweet and kindhearted, always polite and listening to what I had to say. We went different places and continued to learn a great deal about each other. He told me about his younger brothers and sisters and how he loved them. We discussed his illness, and he told me how painful it was as a child. My heart went out to him. It was not out of pity but rather out of empathy. The last thing I wanted to hear was how he was physically suffering.

I can recall one special moment in October when he fell ill. It was around 9:00 PM. He had a fever, and I can remember walking down the hallway of my dormitory, Marian Hall. I had gone to the restroom with a paper towel to wet with hot water. While there, all I could think of was that I did not want the water to be too hot. I adjusted it to the right temperature, wet the towel, and proceeded back to my dorm room. I placed the towel on his forehead for about two minutes and then gently kissed the spot that I had just taken the towel away from. Although he tried to hide it, there was no denying the glow of the smile on his face.

Throughout our relationship, we experienced such an enormous physical and mental connection. The mere mention of his name would create a feeling of weakness in me. Although I was eighteen and he was twenty-two, the force was so strong that I could look into his eyes and go on a journey around the world without needing a passport. He had a unique and original sense of humor and thought outside the box. We shared the same destiny number, the most compatible of Chinese signs, as well as the only two astrology signs that are governed by Mercury, which meant we had the same type of outlook upon life.

We made each other laugh with our witty comments. Often, mental stimulation had a priority in our talks over honesty and truth.

One day, while chatting online, he told me, "Thanks to you and what's on top of your head, there's a poor horse somewhere freezing his ass off."

"Only someone who is hung like a horse can make a reference to one. So refer to a miniature pony from now on," I replied.

We both laughed.

"I can't type that fast," I said.

"That's right, those Lee press-ons!"

"Lol," I replied, which means "laugh out loud."

We did not need to become physically intimate for an orgasm to occur. Truthfully, we never truly explored that side of our relationship because communication was our intimacy. Our love for words, ideas, and thoughts is what brought us together. However, I would soon learn that this factor was not strong enough to keep us together.

"It's too serious for me to be honest." That was the response I received. After waiting for close to a month to hear back from him, I was confronted with such a confusing reply. I kindly and politely asked for him to translate that phrase into English because I just did not understand. He advised me that he did not really know what love was and asked me if I knew. I informed him that I indeed knew, so could he please let me be the spokesperson for my heart and emotions. Although I wanted to believe his supposed inability to define love, I was reluctant to actually accept his words. This was a very intelligent man who gradu-ated cum laude with a BS in computer science. I somehow deciphered his BS to mean he did not feel the same way I felt for him.

Some time after that conversation, to my dismay and shock, I discov-ered that he had slept with someone I was fairly close to. This was rumored to have happened during our relationship. Although I understood that a man has his needs, when we first entered into the relationship I explained to him how we could not become physically intimate with each other until we built a foundation that was strong enough to handle intimacy. I had a desire for the basis of our relationship to be more than just plunging off of the plateau of bodily pleasures into ecstasy. I wanted it to be a place where we could fulfill each other mentally.

He seemed to respect and agree with this. In fact, that is what he told me. However, in due time, I would come to learn this was just a front. Thus going outside the boundaries of our relationship for sexual pleasure only demonstrated his weakness for easy access to a pussycat. And as if that was not the icing on the cake, he not only impregnated a woman before we got together, but he also had another son. Somehow he failed to mention just how busy his little toy soldiers had actually been, declaring war and occupying territory in the time preceding our involvement.

My mind was confused. It felt as though I was in a maze that had no exits. Somehow I wished and hoped this was just a bad nightmare, and I would magically wake-up with any memory of this completely erased. But time elapsed, and the thoughts remained. The loyalty and love I had for him were used as toilet paper to shit on and dispose of. I was officially flushed down the toilet. It never once entered my mind to go outside the realms of our relationship. All I could think about was how I could have known that a companionship that took some time to develop was built upon a foundation of lies and deceit.

Lo and behold, the torment continued. Soon after, rather than referring to me as Mercedes, he used words cunt and bitch.

"I hope you die a slow death," he told me one day.

"What? I will not tolerate this nonsense, you pathetic piece of a penis," I replied.

Although I did not mean what I said, saying that made me feel so damn good. After this exchange of words, much time passed until we spoke again. If I had known that our love for communication would evolve into a destructive way to harm and diminish our consideration, compassion, and uplifting for one another, I would have never considered entering into a relationship with him. But in order to learn and reveal the truth, sometimes we must first experience things for ourselves. Experience remains the best teacher.

On June 31, 2004, I received a note from him. The words were harsh, but the message was even harsher.

It stated, "I don't think you know this but you have nothing that I want. I am in no way attracted to you. Never, not even on your death-bed would I want to see you. You would have to be the last woman on this earth to get anything from me. So from now on, don't im me and don't text me. I am marrying someone else. You are not attractive to me at all. Back in college, when there were slim pickings, you weren't even that attractive to me. You know, if it wasn't for a bet that someone made with me, I would have never got at you. So leave it alone and leave me alone. After all, I don't want to have to give your information to someone to really come and check you. And I don't think that you want her to come and check you I would say it was nice knowing you, but that would be a lie."

A couple of days later, while navigating the Internet, I received an instant message from him. I was not in the mood to have a conversation, but I did anyways.

"Did you send me a text about a red teddy bear?"

"No," I replied.

"Are you sure?"

"Positive."

"You know it could have been you, but you didn't play your cards right. You never bought me anything. She got me a motorcycle, and I got her a ring."

"I don't believe you," I said.

"I'm serious. She makes me feel the way no other girl has. We spend all of our time together, and she's stable. We've planned the wedding to be on September sixteenth. I want you to be there so give me your address, and I will send you an invitation."

"How old is she?"

"She's twenty-seven. She's been married before and has two children. I actually just moved in with her."

"I fucking hate you," I repeated this five times.

"Why are you mad? You want it to be you and not her?"

"No. That has nothing to do with it. It's going to ruin our friendship."

"That's bullshit and you know it. You know there's nothing but love here for you. There's someone out there for you. I'm not that one. You nagged me a lot. You are so difficult. I cannot deal with all of that. I need someone who is going to be my girl and not try to be my mother."

"Whatever. I have to go."

After that I could not speak. I knew that I had to stop talking to him.

My heart died that day. There was a certain numbness. I felt so awful and the desire to isolate myself from the world and everyone in it became urgent. Although that weak part of my body wanted to crawl into a corner and just die, my other half wanted to run up and do a Rambo on him and his girl. However, prison green has never been a flattering color nor was the thought of sharing a six-by-nine-inch steel cubicle with a woman five times my size. So I managed to maintain a cool and level head.

As soon as complete irrationality was taken out of the picture, brace yourself for this, I continuously called, e-mailed, and sent him instant and text messages. That's right, it was stupidity at its best. I felt like a drug addict. He was my drug. I was addicted to his mind, to his words. No matter how harsh his words were, if they were directed toward me, regardless of the manner, it made me feel special. Knowing that he was speaking to me, my heart began to race. I began to crave more of what he offered. Besides, I loved this man. And because I usually do not experience love, when I feel it, I yearn to hold on tight and never to let go.

Both my head, body, and heart were in a game of tug-of-war. Before he entered into my life, it was so easy for me to make the right decisions. It was easy for me to think with my mind. But as soon as love struck me, all of this changed. My head wanted me to go right, but my heart wanted me to go left. My head pressured me to do what I needed to, whereas my heart provoked me to do what I wanted to. If I allowed my head to win this struggle, my heart would ultimately feel betrayed.

Somewhere along this internal struggle, I knew I had to stay away from him. But I also knew that along with this, there would be withdrawal. I was certain I would begin to miss him and think about him all over again. I knew that if I did not take action quickly, this situation would get the worst of me. I did not want love to continue to drive my body insane. I wanted love to get the best of me and but also allow me to become a better person. Could I forget his confession that he was only with me because of a bet that he had made? Could I forget how he told me that I was never attractive to him? I knew this nonsense was never going to magically disappear and erase itself from my memory. I therefore decided to hell with my heart and let it suffer. Somehow I knew this suffering could be no worse than what I had already endured.

It was during this time that I sat back and reminisced on my life. The relationship with my father and other male figures came to the forefront of my mind. Mother figures and role models entered into my mind, and I was reminded of the love others had given and shown to me. My childhood and the way I was raised entered into my mind. I began to analyze myself. "Did I love myself for my differences?" was a question I needed to answer.

I had always avoided those questions, but I knew that within my five-feet-two-inch body, there lay some insecurities. I never cried. I never expressed emotions. In fact, on many occasions, all I would know was that something was bothering me, but I never would acknowledge its cause. Where was the pain coming from? I did not have an answer to these questions because I had a need to avoid direct confrontation. I did not want to confront any type of weakness that I had. I did not want to trigger anything that would make me upset. So as a result of this avoidance, I hid my heart from myself and others.

The years progressed, and I began to relate spending money with self-worth. During my teenage years, I became dependent upon materialism to make me feel better about myself. I used colored contacts, hoping to turn a blind eye to what was really going on. Hazel, then gray, then blue, became my color of choice. Because I was so afraid to embrace my unique individuality, somehow I thought that the money that went into those brand-name jeans, shirts, and shoes would make me feel important and of worth.

My family loved me to an enormous degree, but it was love for myself that was sometimes lacking. Although my biological mother was not around, my aunt, who was my mother in heart and spirit, was always there. I did not have a harsh childhood. My grandmother and aunt did a very wonderful job providing for me. They were my sole providers. It was the father-daughter relationship that led me into stormy waters. And although the love was still strong, my father and I did not have the greatest bond.

I thought about my childhood surroundings. The community I was raised in was not the best, but I refused to become a product of that community. I came to realize that it is not the community but it's the family in that community—immediate and extended—which ultimately dictate one's direction in a life. In fact, those are the two most important factors for success. If the home is full of love, warmth, and positive energy, then that will override the negativity that surrounds that home. If the individual is determined and motivated to pursue and achieve their dreams, then the devastating atmosphere they grow up in will not get in the way of achieving success. For it is an individual's right to choose, which enables that person to either win or lose. And it is that ability which will prove to be either the most rewarding or destructive right of them all.

I somehow knew that having these burdens weighing down my heart would make it harder for me to progress and find internal happiness. Because of all of these burdens and having so much emotional baggage at such a young age, I felt overcome with dilemma. I did not want to be out of the game before it had even begun.

*I needed closure, and I knew that I had it in me to discover uncondi-
tional love for myself. I'd find this out by appreciating myself more. This
information would allow me to solve this equation of turmoil. I knew
that finding love within myself and never allowing that love to be jeop-
ardized by the opinions of others—because I did not match their image
of beauty—would give me the courage to stand up for myself.*

*In order to repair the damage in my life, I first began to change how
I think. I rejected my negative thoughts and embraced a more positive
outlook. I started to realize that in order to be worthy, I did not have to
wear my worth. I learned how to say no to the negative and say yes to
information this breakup was trying to show me about my life and love.
I began to appreciate the privileges life had awarded me, rather than to
dwell on what I felt life had taken from me. I rejected the bitterness and
anger that my past had inflicted on me. I began to embrace spiritual
and inner peace. I began to embrace my individuality. I began to accept
and love myself for the person I was.*

*If my words could touch him today, I would say, "How you could be
so cold is beyond me. I gave you one of the most important organs that I
possess: my heart. I gave you the most important emotion that my body
has to offer: my love. Love is not a game. Love is not to be used or
abused. Love is not to be defamed. I loved you in a way that I never
thought possible. I never knew that my heart had the ability to beat for
only one person. You may look at this as being weak, but the ability to
express what your heart feels is anything but weak. It shows strength. It
shows your human ability to experience and not give a damn about
what anyone has to say. Besides, every strong woman experiences at least
one weak moment at some point in time. However, it is how she
bounces back that is the true indicator of not only her strength, but the
quantity of her strength. And yes, I will not deny it. Bitterness begs me to
say that I hate you, but strength compels me to wish you the best that
love and life have to offer. And I have finally decided to side with
strength."*

To this day, I still do feel a certain, although small, level of disappointment. I am not disappointed that he found a Mitsubishi more appealing than a Mercedes. Rather, the direction of this disappointment points to my inability to realize that the best gifts come in the smallest of packages. This disappointment lies in my inability to stand up for myself and be that strong woman and walk away sooner. Indeed, he only treated me the way I allowed him to. He only spoke to me the way I allowed him to. I never wanted to be a fool for love. I never wanted to be a fool in love. I tried so hard to avoid being foolish. And although I tried so hard to prevent it, it still happened. Since then, I have made a contract with myself. The primary term of that agreement is this: no more and never again will I ever allow for my body to be a victim to nonsense.

At the end of this journey, the answer to a very important question finally revealed itself to me. For some time, Tina, as well as I, yearned to know, "What's love got to do with it?" Although Tina discovered the answer to this question some time ago, I recently discovered mine. The revelation was like a slow but steady unveiling. Still, the light managed to make its way to my eyes. Unlike the past, I refused to put on shades and look away into the darkness. So what was the answer, inquiring minds want to know? Well, inquiring minds, inquire no more. Love has not a damn thing to do with it when it involves loving someone who shows no love to you. But this love has every damn thing to do with it when it involves embracing and cherishing the person who lives within you.

3

Love
2
Be
Defined

Love 2 be discovered is love 2 be defined. Love 2 be defined is guaranteed 2 blow your mind. Love 2 be divine within the heart and mind is love that cannot be denied. Love 2 be denied is 2 be disguised, used in vain and defamed on behalf of the essence of its name. Love 2 be dismissed allows for you 2 miss out on the joy of love itself. LOve is Valued Eternally is love truly defined.

Do I really want to be loved or do I just want love to be near for the sake of having it around? Do I really want to be loved because I feel as though I need it, want it, or am I afraid of having to live without it? Does love really have a meaning to me, or is it just an emotion that is no different than like or lust? If I am loved, am I willing to show that love back, or am I just going to selfishly keep it to myself? Do I love unconditionally or does my love have limits? If I am never loved, will I not love myself? Will I ultimately come to hate myself because if no one loves me, then why should I love myself?

Are my breasts the only thing worth being loved? Is my ass the only thing worth being loved? Should the rest of my body, including my mind—where the real me lies—just be avoided, neglected, and not loved in favor of aesthetic value? Am I worth being hugged and appreciated not because of what lies in between my thighs but for what lies within my heart? Is my vagina the only thing worth being cherished? Is that where the essence of the love I receive really lies?

Do I really know love in its most positive and enriching form? Have I seen this type of love? Was I exposed to a loving relationship between my mother and father? Did I witness those moments of tenderness and affection, the nonstop words of encouragement that my father showed not only me and my siblings, but to my mother? Did I not only hear the words "I love you" from his mouth, but was I shown that love through action? Has he always been there for me, through times when I really needed his presence and words of wisdom? Has he always been there for the woman who lay with him and sacrificed her life for the upbringing of his children?

To answer the preceding questions is to unveil love defined in its most positive and enriching form.

I am quite sure many minds are wondering, what does a twenty-two-year-old female know about love? Yes, I am no certified relationship expert. I do not have a PhD. A higher education institution has never granted me an honorary doctorate. But through experience, my own personal relationships, and relationships that I have been a third party to—mainly through assisting friends with their battered emotions—have awarded me access into the unknown world of love. It is this knowledge that has awarded me the ability to inform and assist in the definition of love and its effects.

My love for information, observation, and analysis has given me an understanding of human nature. This allows me to gain insights into the behavioral ways and patterns of the no-good man. It is this same awareness that grants me the ability to give further insight and understanding into the issues that arise within a woman to accept and tolerate his ways. It is this combination, accompanied by analysis and the application of certain personal theories and principles, which gives me insight into a world where definitive answers do not exist.

In my twenty-two years of life, I have come to learn that the greatest and most valuable gift one person can give another is knowledge. For it is only knowledge that can and will be that life jacket to save a soul from the possible devastating pitfalls that await on life's journey. Indeed, I have discovered that my ultimate purpose and life path in this world is to educate and share the knowledge I have been so blessed to acquire because knowledge means nothing if it is selfishly kept to oneself. If I choose to selfishly withhold what I know, then I would be doing the world of women a disservice. I can only provide the information; the choice the reader makes with it is up to her. It is up to the individual to apply it in a positive and enriching manner. If this is neglected, then the gift will be wasted.

This book will introduce and focus upon that notorious emotion called love, specifically in its romantic form. This also happens to be that same emotion which bruises hearts and claims so many victims. Throughout the years, I have come to learn that love is an emotion to be cherished because it can sometimes not be easily felt, recognized, or accepted. And unfortunately, when in love, thinking with the heart often overrides thinking with the head.

Love will make the lips smile when in the presence of the person who has captured the heart. Love can often influence the mind to think of nothing else but intermingling one future with another's. Love can encourage the body to love that individual for their attributes and come to love that person even more for their faults. Frequently, love motivates the body to place trust in the loved one, allowing for the vulnerability of all the negative effects that may result if that trust is taken for granted and abused. Often, love encourages the eyes to look at the loved one—even if they may have the physical features of a rodent—and still believe they are the most attractive person they have ever come across. Love can provoke the body to completely devote and commit itself to maintaining the happiness and well-being of the loved one. Love can also make the body cringe at the very thought of having to live without that person.

Love will sometimes motivate the mind to place the body at risk for HIV and other sexually transmitted diseases. Love within the heart of a woman can sometimes elect the body to be a single mother by raising a child who does not have a father, but rather a sperm donor. Love can often force the mind to think in terms of securing the love that the heart feels, whereas in order to do so, the body becomes willing to secure that relationship regardless of the possible negative side effects. The objective of this enables the blood's ability to be warm and flow toward the heart, thus bringing it happiness. Unfortunately, sometimes good love goes unappreciated. And just like that of a good woman, it must be lost in order to be appreciated.

I happen to know, firsthand, that being in love will definitely make an individual choose not to apply their common sense, intelligence, and all other positive attributes. When there is even a slight assumption that it is being taken advantage of, love can motivate an individual to dress in camouflage and hide behind the bushes like a soldier. Love can also provoke the fingers to continuously call the person's phone with a blocked number just to hear their voice. Positive love will motivate the heart to smile, while negative love will provoke the heart to weep by allowing the mind to be driven into insanity.

There is a common perception of love being blind. Love is believed to disable the eyes from seeing a destructive situation clearly. I believe the opposite. Love has a way of making excuses that condone specific behavior; I believe that the party in love voluntarily chooses to look left when in love because looking in the right direction is too difficult. Looking left allows for the person to continue on with the fantasy because the reality is harsh. Believing that love is blind not only relieves the person of responsibility but it also soothes the guilt and feeling of embarrassment that one will have for allowing the situation to continue.

I refuse to believe that an adult, knowing right from wrong and with knowledge acquired from TV or social interactions, cannot pick up on certain signs and realize how those particular struggles are related to what is occurring in their own backyard. In terms of love and sight, love does not blind us. Love does not make us incompetent or get rid of our intelligence. Instead, love sedates us. It makes us passive. Love makes us optimistic about the validity of the words that come out of the loved one's mouth. Love makes us more forgiving. Love makes us optimistic that change will soon arrive.

Love that is good and enriching will never need to be hidden, and the truth of what is really going on will allow others to automatically see how nurturing the relationship is and extend their admiration. The woman involved in a good relationship will assume her bragging rights and gloat about how good the love truly is. In a relationship that is abusive and bad, the woman will hide and use lies to cover up the problems. The reason for this is simple. The negative relationship will get negative feedback. Those with an outside view will force the mind into reality. They will force the mind out of that fantasy to look at the situation for what it really is: a catastrophe. Therefore, if friends and family have not been told the truth about what is really going on, then something is probably going wrong.

In terms of my love and relationship with the specific man in question, have I ever hit, beat on, or smacked? The answer is no. If that had occurred, this book would be entitled, *Doing Time 4 Homicide*. However, I am a victim of an abused heart. Unfortunately, the wounds of a heart can actually be more devastating than physical abuse. Specifically, heartache quite frequently takes a longer time to heal than physical bruises. Medicine heals physical wounds, requiring no additional effort beyond taking and applying the medicine to receive. But with heartache, much human effort is needed to heal.

Expressing emotions from past experiences generates strength. When those who have experienced pain and heartache become aware of another person who has felt those same emotions, they are empowered to move forward. This can soothe open wounds and prepare them for closure by providing a way to release that long-held anger and tension. The consoling feeling that comes from knowing you are not alone will ultimately allow for a means to find a solution to the problem, not of the no-good man and how to make him good, but of building up the spirit as an individual woman. This will reveal the reason why the woman has long sought to avoid the responsibility that she has as a woman: being strong enough to stand up for herself, leave that negative situation, learn from it, progress, and do the best job in preventing it from happening again.

It is inevitable that difficulties will arise with love. As they do, we should never feel we have been stressed with them but rather blessed with them. For within pain, there is always a blessing or a lesson in disguise that we should never take in vain. The ability to view difficult situations like this does, indeed, take time because anger is the natural reaction to dissatisfaction. Love will come, but please bear in mind that patience is a highly respected virtue. Sometimes we have to climb some steep mountains and overcome great obstacles to reach that high plateau. In the end, we will definitely be compensated for all the suffering and rewarded with the ultimate prize.

Even if the reward is not a life partner, it will be a lifetime's worth of priceless knowledge.

To capture life defined does present some difficulty. As a general rule in both life and love, life is not meant to be fair; it is only meant to be lived. Unfortunately, living within the human flesh does not reward us the privilege that cats have. So we must do the very best with this one-and-only life by living it to the fullest. We must realize life is itself an opportunity and a reward. In order to live and define life, we must take full advantage of what living has to offer, by progressing. Thus, in order to progress, we must view life the way we view walking, by making steps forward, never backward, sideways, or in circles.

In order to live life, we must also bear in mind that the mind leads and the body follows. Once the mind is freed, the body will follow. If we give the mind the chance to think, prove, and demonstrate its capabilities, we will find that it is indeed an extraordinary and powerful place. What we will also discover is that the body will have found the key to unlock the greatest achievements of life. In other words, goals will cease to be dreams and become a true living and breathing reality. But only by way of individual strength, will, and dedication can we set this in motion.

The individual definition of life can sometimes lead the body to an abundance of happiness and a minimal amount of pain. On the contrary, individual experiences can sometimes lead the body in an opposite direction toward the discovery of abundant pain and minimal happiness. However, pain and happiness through experience are a part of the plan. Pains and pleasures are all to be cherished because they help us shape and build individuality. They allow for us to make life something that is distinctive and unique. Our pains and struggles all symbolize what we have been through and define who we are as separate beings. So regardless of the devastation we face, life must and still will go on. Therefore, in the midst of pain, we should not allow life to be plagued by bitterness and pass us by.

Throughout life's journey toward love's discovery, I know everyone will agree that love is an amazing emotion, but it can also be destructive. Notice the word *can*, for this is only if we allow it to be. But the heart of a woman shares a certain commonality, which also happens to be our advantage in times of difficulty. In general, this similarity is defined by the emotional obstacles and challenges we experience. These are the same situations that allow for the body of a woman to gain strength, increasing its tolerance and endurance to combat struggles and obstacles that will continue to confront us in a world that males dominate.

So, my dear woman, in times of despair and solace, when you feel as though your capacity to handle obstacles has departed and your life and love for self are still not defined, always remember that the heart and spirit of a woman, in all their ferocity and undying will to endure, will never let you down nor abandon you. For it is this same spirit that will somehow find a way to carpe diem, or seize the day and redeliver your love and life back to its original owner: **YOU**.

4

A Woman, a Heart, and the Emotions That Run Through It

The following dialogue depicts a conversation between a mother and her eleven-year-old daughter. The mother explains to her child the worth and purpose of a woman, as well as the meaning of life in general.

"Child, daughter, my young princess, you will grow up to be a queen. From a girl to a woman you will become, and the thing that differentiates the two is that a woman can and will always be able to stand on her own two feet, not kneel or bow, but use the strength of her body to get up and stand up for what she believes and wants out of life. A woman will never compromise the integrity, respect, and love she has for herself. As a woman, you will never be embarrassed to say no to those who refuse to respect you and your beliefs. You will think with the mind that God has given you, and never allow for someone else to think for

you. You will not just exist. You will live your life in a straight line, not a circle."

Her daughter replies, *"What does that mean, Mom: to live your life in a circle or to live your life in a straight line? What is it to exist or to live?"*

"Child, this means you will not end at the same point at which you began. This means you will progress from A by achieving the goals you set in life. You will end at Z, fully accomplishing whatever you wish and seek to do. As you grow up, live, learn, and feel with your own body, you will come to realize that some people only exist. They do not live. Just because you have a pulse does not mean you're living. Some people eat, sleep, work, and pay bills. This constitutes the true meaning of existing. Your life revolves in a circle, going from day to day in the same motion, the same pattern. Existing means not realizing your full potential or taking advantage of opportunities that life has awarded you."

Her mother continues the lecture.

"In order to die, you must first live. In order to end your life, you must first have started it and lived it with no regrets about the decisions you have made. In order to be satisfied with the end of your life, you must have lived the beginning and middle of your life to your fullest potential. And to truly live life is to educate yourself. To live life is when you die to live, not live to die. It is to breathe and realize that every breath you take is for a reason. And it is with the energy and life supplied by the oxygen from this breath that you must and will reach your ultimate potential and never take life for granted."

Her mother continues by describing to her a woman's worth.

"My child, one day I sat down by my grandmother and was given this same lecture. This was a very long time ago. But one of the most valuable stories she has ever told me was how she was once taken into a meat market by her mother, your great, great-grandmother."

Her mother interrupts the story.

"Hey, you're not falling asleep on me, are you?"

"No, Mom!"

"Now, you're not thinking about running away, are you? Because you know your mother has a way of running off at the mouth. My mother once told me that if a tongue had a bone, mine would have been broken in a hundred places!"

"Please, just finish the story!"

"Now you see all of the meat in this market?" stated my grand-mother, Dorothy.

"Yes," my mother replied.

"Which do you think is the most valuable piece?" she asked.

"Now, she did not mean this in terms of price. She meant it in terms of essence. My mother told me that she did not know what to say at first, so she just looked at the different prices and pieces of the body parts in the market. My mother then pointed to the most expensive piece, which was the leg of an animal. Now obviously, that would have been any child's choice considering that it was the most expensive piece, at $1.00. Well you probably don't know but back in the good ole' days, the prices were much cheaper than they are today. But her mother told her, 'No, my child. The leg may be the most expensive, but the most valuable piece is the center cut of the animal, which is what you sit on, my daughter.' Now this is not the cushion of a chair but it is the cushioning in between your thighs. That's the most valuable prize. That is the essence of wom-anhood and is something that should always be valued. It cannot just be handed out to any hungry individual. Now do not take this message and use it to think that what lies down below is all that you are worth. The definition of your womanhood is not restricted to what is in between your legs. But rather it is a combination of that along with what lies in between your eyes, and that, my dear, is your mind. That is the overall essence of womanhood. The cushioning in between your legs allows for you to bring life into the world, but what lies upstairs, allows you to elevate your own individual position. It allows for you to make

something positive out of your name. For what lies in between your thighs does not separate and distinguish you as a real woman or an individual. Only what lies upstairs can do that."

Her daughter replies, "Cushion, Mom! You're funny."

As her mother concludes the lecture, she states:

"As you live your life, my child, you will feel with your heart. But be very careful, and make sure not to allow your heart to think for you. Many people, men, women, and just society in general, will seek to test and challenge the commitment you have to your ethics to see how you stand against challenges. But you will succeed, my darling, and you will grow strong and prove, not only to others, but to yourself, that you are a strong young woman with the potential to achieve many great things. You are a young queen, my child. And the one thing that a queen deserves is a king. And when your time has come, you will find your king."

Before she places a soft kiss atop of her daughter's forehead, she states, "I love you, my young queen."

Her daughter responds, "I love you too, Mom!"

Is it the breast, the vagina, the ovaries with their ability to conceive, or the X chromosome substituted for a Y, that truly defines a woman? The answer is absolutely not, times four. What truly defines a woman is her strength, which is the cohesive glue and backbone of every family, in every culture, and on every continent. This is the same strength that single-handedly raises children, providing for them even when the sperm donor has decided to disappear. This is the same strength that works day and night to maintain the household. And what is strength? I define strength as the ability to persevere and overcome all obstacles in order to construct a certain level of immunity to harm. This will allow for the body to claim victory by fighting off other infectious and detrimental factors that try to weaken it.

An ingredient that also contributes to the definition of a woman is emotion. Women are more emotional than men. In fact, emotional differences between the male and female become very evident at an early age. When a little girl falls down, she will often cry. However, when a little boy falls down, he is most likely not to. In fact, this same emotional response continues as the years progress. In times of sorrow and pain, a woman will often cry without fear of being labeled as weak.

In times when the heart feels love, a woman will confess her love. A woman will also be unafraid to confer with her girlfriends about love issues or skim through the pages of hundreds of women's magazines about men and relationships. However, men will often demonstrate the opposite. They will usually refrain from being overly emotional or emotionally expressive in the presence of a woman. Often, they will not talk about their feelings with friends. There is always some fear, usually of being labeled as weak or gay, that can create this avoidance.

Women have intense experiences that activate their emotional side. From PMS to childbirth, these lay the foundation for an increase in sensitivity when it comes to other areas of life. This leads women to not only experience relationships differently but often to respond to love and pain differently. Thus, when these emotions are felt, there is usually more intensity. This very premise gives way to the phrase, "Hell hath no fury like a woman scorned." Popular belief states that the more emotional partner is usually the more attached and weaker of the two. Often, this is the woman.

The fact that the word *woman* indicates strength is undeniable. From the Woman's Suffrage Movement to our persistent fight for equal rights and sexual harassment legislation in the workplace, as well as other pivotal historical events in which women were at the forefront, there are many demonstrations of that fact.

Another undeniable fact is that to be a woman in a male-dominated world is no easy task. This has an even greater truth within the workforce, because many men are still skeptical that a woman can be as efficient and productive as her male counterpart. The origin of this skepticism stems from an archaic **men**tality that limits the woman's purpose to child rearing and maintaining a household. Although women constantly overcome societal barriers, including that of corporate obstacles, to attain powerful positions as CEOs, attorneys, doctors, these positions will always be in a state of jeopardy because men control the very fate of every industry.

Those who base a woman's worth and potential solely on procreation, sexual attributes, and the ability to run a household will seek to continuously critique and doubt a woman's intellectual capabilities, as well as her position within the workforce. However, this perception of limited potential is inaccurate and doesn't recognize the accomplishments of women within this society. Naturally, this chauvinistic mentality flows from the workforce into a relationship. In fact, the origin of this attitude sometimes begins in childhood from the observation of the traditional roles and duties of the mother and father.

Corporate forces will always mandate women to assert worthiness. Women will always be in a position to prove their presence in the corporate environment. Women must prove their presence is not just because of a need to satisfy the element of diversity within the workplace and comply with legislation. There is a constant struggle to prove that women possess an intellectual and endurance capacity that, in many cases, surpass that of men. Who else can bring home the bacon and cook it, and maintain the household too? Being able to perform those specific duties requires an innate skill that a man just does not have. This innate skill is neither up for purchase, nor can it be acquired through a university.

Our society and others are primary examples of the exploitation and subordination of women. American culture promotes pimps, producers of porn videos, and music videos in which women bare all to entice the male audience. These specific industries make a profit off of degrading the very organs which are the major reason for their existence: the woman, vagina, breast, and rear end. In the corporate world, women get paid less to do the same exact job as men. With marriage, the woman's surname changes by deleting her original name and then adding the man's last name onto her first name. On the contrary, the man's identity stays the same. The birth of a child presents no difference. The woman does all of the work and the man gets all of the credit by having his surname added onto the child's name.

Some of the most extreme forms of oppression originate in the Red Sea region. In fact, history has dictated oppression of women as a traditionally upheld practice of high value. In some areas, the woman must be covered from head to toe at all times or she is stoned to death. There is no trial. She is proven to be guilty, not because of the incriminating evidence against her, but because of her gender. Polygamy, which allows for the husband to have many wives, is also a traditional practice. However, if the wife dares to go outside of the confines of her marriage for some additional sexual activity, she will automatically find herself at death's door. In some areas, women cannot check into a hotel without a male family member. They are also prohibited from driving cars.

Japanese society represents a place where there is no government intervention for the protection of women's rights. In the workforce there are no sexual harassment laws that penalize a man for over-stepping his boundaries. Rape legislation dictates that in order for a woman to prove that she has been a victim of rape, it must be proven that the force used was so extreme that it prevented her from resisting. The difficulty of proving rape increases when the government defines sex to include a certain degree of violence.

All this illustrates how history has created the groundwork for the current and continual oppression and exploitation of women. And although there is a gray area, specifically in regions where religion governs the way of life, use of this higher divinity justifies the subordination of women. This allows for women to be kept in a submissive and powerless position. The objective is to keep women at an inferior state.

Language also seeks to reinforce and confirm this idea. Specifically, the words *bitch* and *ho* were given new definitions from their original meanings and applied to decrease the woman's value and significance as a traditionally strong and powerful image. When a man calls a female a bitch, he is not telling her that she is a woman; he is telling her that she is a female dog. And in society, the worth of an animal will always be less than that of a human.

The men who willingly participate in the degradation of women contribute to furthering its purpose. And what is the overall purpose of this practice? To intercept a woman's thought process and make her believe she is worthless and has limited potential outside of her physical attributes. There is also the underlying goal of weakening her true womanhood. Her actions will begin to reflect her mental attitude because as soon as this belief is incorporated into the thought process, her body will begin to do and act as her worth, which is like the words themselves, little to nothing. This deception may ultimately eliminate her ability to exhibit strength and make her more tolerant of nonsense from the male.

The essence of a woman's worth is in the creation of life. We bring life into the world. We nurture that life. A woman's legs are the ones arched in that delivery room. It is that same woman who pushes continuously until the head, legs, and arms of the baby appear. It is the mother who provides for that child, not only with her breast, but with her love, security, and unyielding devotion. It is the mother who is a powerful, perhaps the most powerful, image and role model of a woman that her child will interact with. Therefore, all women must take heed and seek to be that ideal and the best woman they can possibly be. If a mother happens to choose the opposite path, her son or daughter may become that future no-good man or no-good woman of society.

Inside of every woman is the heart. And the heart is the most delicate organ within the body. It also happens to be one of the most important organs, transporting blood through the arteries and veins to sustain life. Besides this vital medical function, the heart also allows for an individual to feel and experience the magnitude of human emotion. One can hear, touch, smell, taste, and see. However, the heart will allow for one to feel emotions.

In addition to the heart's most vital purpose of sustaining life, its other significant purpose is to allow all humans to experience the depth of true and real love. And to live a life without love is to never experience the complete depth of life at all. Confined within this organ is also the ability to feel pain and happiness resulting from like, lust, or love. Although these three Ls are very familiar experiences, only love has its origin within the heart. Love is the only condition that originates within the heart and has a permanent place. And not just any type of love—because love in its romantic form is not a permanent condition, since we can fall in and out of love on various occasions—but true love. Lust and like have no true emotional significance compared to love. Sometimes like and lust try to disguise themselves as love, confusing those involved in a romantic relationship.

Love, in its most true and genuine form, is a mixture of spiritual, mental, and unselfish dedication. This concept happens to be very difficult for some to grasp. This can be expected when some of us have a distorted view of what love really is supposed to be. Love is not up for sale through gifts. Love is not defined by money, the size of a penis, or the endurance capacity of a vagina. How many orgasms can be achieved within the matter of an hour does not define how much love is present. Love includes appreciation, compassion, and respect.

In terms of sight and love, can love really be accessed by sight? Love is much more than physical appearance. If the eyes see an appealing body, then "lust at first sight" is the more valid term. Love, itself, is initiated from the head and then works its way down to occupy the heart. When two people begin to learn about one another, their minds are allowed to make a connection by finding shared interests or principles of life. This will allow for the interest to continue on in a downward motion and occupy the heart. If it begins in the reverse motion, working from below the waist up, then lust may be confused as love. Love itself will be given a distorted and superficial meaning if its sole basis is upon a below-the-waist or on-the-surface basis.

In order to feel love, we must realize that the first step is to explore the individual. The true individual is located above the waist. Below the waist we are all the same. Nothing distinguishes one from another. As we begin to experience deep emotions and fall in love with the true individual, which is in the heart and mind, then we can extend love to that person. Once both portions of the body are mutually satisfied, then the total blending can continue on in a downward motion of sexual satisfaction below the waist.

Everything in this world has a purpose. In order to experience pleasure, we must first experience pain. In order to truly value pleasure, pain must have had some place within the body. This is necessary in order to take full advantage of the thirst that true love quenches once it arrives within the heart. Nonetheless, it is not just any type of love. It is not the negative love that someone can have for an addiction that contributes to self-destruction. This specific type of love is positive and promotes self-growth. It expands our own individual horizons, increasing our respect for life and all it has to offer: family, children, education, spirituality, etc. Positive love is where true, real love lies. For it is true love that fulfills everything we desire. Love only fulfills a majority of what we hope for.

Those who have never come into contact with love, specifically in the romantic form, may experience difficulty in recognizing it. Once it shows up within the heart, it may be hard to accept. There may also be an urge to rebel and lash out against this foreign feeling. The vulnerability may be very difficult to cope with. However, the feeling is amazing and we can come to learn so much from it. We can come to learn a new appreciation. We can come to learn the value of love and not just its price. We can come to see, firsthand, the reality of its potential and the overwhelming, amazing effect that it has over the body. The existence of these other emotions allows us to be able to distinguish between positive and negative feelings, arrive at love, and partake upon a new view of life.

Everyone wants and needs love, but is everyone deserving of it? Is everyone capable of giving it? The answer is no and no. Neither is everyone deserving of love, in terms of its romantic form, nor is everyone capable of displaying the nurturing type of love that the body truly needs. How can one possibly love if one has never been exposed to love in its positive, growth-promoting, and nurturing form? When we speak of displaying love, we must realize it is not the affectionate part that constitutes love. Anyone who is mobile can give the hugs, kisses, and sweet talk. That is the easy part. But true love comes in the form of encouragement and support, both in the physical and emotional sense and none other. Some are incapable of displaying this.

Often, it is that temporary feeling of lust or more permanent feeling of longing and what we feel and think to be love that can impair our ability to adequately think. We must come to realize that the body is a temple deserving nothing less than worship. We have one and only one life and body, therefore we must never mistreat it or allow for another to do so. It is within the body that the mind lies. This same mind is the one element that leads us in the journey of defining who we are and allows us to think and explore our thoughts. Without these two significant components, there is no life, no woman, no heart, and no emotion.

Once the end of the day has arrived, the two Ls will be long gone. Time will have allowed for lust and like to escape from the body. There may be a slight memory of the two but no permanent attachment. This will lead one to find that the only emotion of any value will be that final and most important L: love. Ultimately, it is not the love for someone else that really matters. What will be the most significant is the love that we have for the reflection we see in the mirror. It is to love thyself and all that comes with the body that truly is the greatest love of all.

5

Relationship Versus Realationship

Trust + Honesty + Sincerity + Love + Commitment + Genuine Intent + Dedication + Faith + Spirituality + Compassion + Consideration + Open Communication + Respect + Loyalty + Monogamy + Understanding + Integrity +Mental Connection + Friendship + Devotion = the key ingredients in forming, not a relationship, but a realationship.

One can have all of the above qualities with another, but what about the qualities that an individual has with themselves?

What is the value of trust when I give into lies and begin not to have belief in my own ability to do what is best for me? Trust has no value. What does being honest with another mean if I am not honest with myself about who I am? Honesty means nothing. What does being sincere to another mean if I am not true to defining who I am and discovering my potential in this lifetime? Sincerity means nothing. What is the value of love when I love another so much that I show no care toward who I am? Love has no value. What is the value of commitment when I am so devoted to helping another that I do not pledge myself to defining my own life, discovering that strength, and trying to be all that I can possibly be? Commitment has no value. What does going into a relationship with genuine intent mean if my interaction with myself is built upon a foundation of deceit and lies about who I am? Genuine intent means nothing.

What is the value of dedication when I am so dedicated to another that I forget I exist? Dedication has no value. What is the value of faith when I put all of it into another but none into my own ability to achieve and progress? Faith has no value. What does having a spiritual connection with another mean if I do not embrace and practice holiness and forgiveness within my own life? Spirituality means nothing. What is the value of compassion for another if I do not demonstrate a sympathy that creates a desire to help myself? Compassion has no value. What does consideration mean to another if I have little regard for my own emotions and all that I go through? Consideration means nothing.

What is the value of open communication with another about my feelings when I close my ears and mouth to the truth about how I really feel about who I am? Open communication has no value. What is the value of respect when I show so much to him but little to myself and those who truly love me? Respect has no value. What is the value of loyalty when I am loyal to him but show little loyalty to my own body and insult it with neglect? Loyalty has no value. What is the value of monogamy when I give fidelity to him but do not receive it in return? Monogamy has no value. What does understanding of another mean if I fail to grasp the meaning of who I am as a woman and my reality? Understanding means nothing.

What is the value of integrity when I have principles in mind but do not apply them in life? Integrity has no value. What does establishing a mental connection with another mean if I have never embraced or explored the depths of my mind to locate my passions, desires, and potential in life? A mental connection means nothing. What does friendship with another mean if I cannot be a friend and an advocate for my own best interests when despair and negativity have crept into my life? Friendship has no value. What does devotion mean to another if I show *no support to who I am and my ability to grow as a woman? Devotion means nothing.*

Ultimately, a realationship has no value and means nothing to another if one has not yet to form a realationship with oneself.

Relationship and realationship sound the same but they do not necessarily mean the same. Many may view these terms as inter-changeable and substitute one for the other. However, the reality is that only one indicates that the other is present. A realationship is a relationship but in a higher form. The relationship, however, does not necessarily indicate that a realationship has been formed. None-theless, the relationship, when given time to develop, along with effort and dedication on behalf of both parties, can be the key to unlock the gateway of some day forming its higher and deeper form.

A relationship, in the romantic sense, is commonly known as a level of togetherness between two people who share some type of interest in one another. As a result, these two individuals will seek to establish a union based upon this interest. A relationship can exist in the form of a marriage or dating. There are no restrictions. The analysis exists on a psychological level. It involves the mental atti-tude of both participants. The existence of commitment, sincerity, involvement, and intent will also be questionable. Within the rela-tionship, lies may be abundant. However, it is not the relationship that people should aim for; it is the realationship.

The initial stage of forming a relationship may involve one party having good intentions while the other may not. The aim for us get-ting to know each other can sometimes be to actually form a good relationship. However, some do not turn out as such. Some will begin as good relationships but end up as bad ones. Other relation-ships may start out as bad but be wonderful. We never know. None-theless, if the effort to make it better is present within both parties, along with the most significant qualities of honesty, sincerity, and fidelity, then there is a possibility of success.

In general terms, two individuals can base a relationship upon anything: infatuation, love, lust, materialism, or the selfish pursuit of personal wealth and security that their partner can provide. The formation of a realationship occurs when there is an emphasis on more than just engaging in romance. A realationship occurs when there is an overall sense of realness and all of the other virtues. That can sometimes be difficult to achieve because the nature of the human is rooted in an instinct that drives one toward the fulfillment of self first and them last. A realationship initiates an ultimate level of togetherness.

The fulfillment of the term realationship is based upon whether there is the existence of sincerity, as well as the level of this sincerity on the part of both partners. Honesty is also important. The intent of both parties must not be rooted in an ulterior motive besides wanting to create something worthy with the party of interest. In the realationship, there are no masks to disguise one's true self because there is no use for them. Halloween is not an everyday event because these individuals are themselves, in their true and genuine form. In order to have a realationship, the level of realness must be equal between the two parties. There must be equal and complete honesty, sincerity, and motivation.

Sex can be the yeast of a relationship. However, the foundation or main ingredient that forms the basis of a realationship is never based upon sex. The relationship, as well as the realationship, can be either on an intimate or non-intimate level. If it does involve intimacy, then a relationship does not automatically mean monogamy. The realationship symbolizes a special companionship that is way above average because it includes fidelity. It involves a meeting of the hearts and not just the parts.

In order to establish a realationship, the individuals must experience a blending of the mind, body, and spirit. This partnership involves an exploration of the mind that then extends down to heart. This interest then maneuvers its way down to explore the intimate parts. The order does not necessarily have to follow this pattern, but the most important thing is that a connection with all parts will be made. It has to be much more than just a physical connection because this alone will not fulfill the test for strength. It must be more than lust because this alone will not pass the test for longevity. Both qualities are not enough to stand the test of time and overcome the obstacles that get in the way of every relationship. The realationship is meant to be long-lasting, assuming the individuals are willing to continuously apply the specific qualities to the realationship. When this fails and one of the qualities of the realationship has been betrayed, then the realationship converts back into a relationship. There may be much difficulty for it to return back into a realationship. In the back of the betrayed person's mind, there may always be the fear that the person will seek to betray them once again.

Infidelity can destroy trust and replace it with distrust. This can destroy the mental connection and replace it with mental confusion. This destroys the idea of a mental rapport because the mind has now erupted into a confused state and will no longer focus upon engaging with the betrayer in an open and natural fashion. This destroys the idea of loyalty and truth, replacing it with disloyalty and lies. The interaction will become cautious and restrictive. Once those components have dissolved, the realationship will gradually dissolve too.

Human nature sometimes leads the body to embrace negative urges and instincts. The idea of survival and self-preservation, in terms of pursuing all that can increase the quality of life and bring happiness, can often motivate some to actions that satisfy the desires of self while hurting others in the process. This can also lead to overindulgence and greed. This will leave open-ended questions in the back of the mind, especially within the confines of a relationship. This may trigger speculations about the genuineness of intent of one party by the other. If this issue goes unresolved and is allowed to turn into bitterness and pain, then what may result is an act of vengeance. If the two individuals allow for these issues to linger without open communication, the relationship will never evolve into a realationship.

The negative traits of human nature reveal themselves within the no-good man's individual nature. As a result, there only lies the possibility of a relationship. It is impossible for a woman to have a realationship with the no-good man. His entire foundation has its roots in false information. The basis of his interaction with a woman is grounded in unauthentic terms. He thrives on being able to deceive, manipulate, and lie. Therefore, the criteria by which a realationship is formed are unable to be fulfilled. This same idea also applies to the no-good woman.

Marriage does not automatically denote that a realationship has been formed. In fact, there may be more of a realationship between a female and male who are not legally united. How can I draw such a conclusion? If marriage denoted a realationship with all of the necessary ingredients, then why is the divorce rate in America so high? If both parties within the relationship exhibit all of the qualities of a realationship, then marriages would last forever, or until one spouse dies. There would also be no use for divorce lawyers, prenuptial agreements, and all of the other legal mechanisms to prepare for the aftermath of a person's lies, deceits, and infidelity.

In terms of relationship versus realationship, there is an emphasis of the realationship above the relationship. This does not mean that the relationship is meant to fail. In any event, there are qualities of the realationship that do not require individual input; some come naturally. Indeed, not everyone may be able to find someone to experience an intense connection with. But with a little adjusting and compromising on some standards, there will always be someone who is at least compatible on the most important levels. Finding a mate is not easy and learning how to make that relationship work may be even harder, but everything requires effort. Thus, if the relationship is workable, then at least it is worth the effort.

In the process of forming a realationship, the most significant thing to keep in mind is that one must first form a realationship with self. We must have a genuine and complete definition of self before we can attempt to get to know and learn about someone else. We must be true to this definition. We must have a clear and accurate vision of where we are going in life: our goals, aspirations, and desires. We must also be honest with ourselves about who we are. We must not paint an imaginary image of our aspirations if we have no intention of achieving those goals. We must not lie or be in denial about the internal issues that cause us pain. We must commit ourselves to resolving these issues. We must do what inspires the heart. We must do what inspires happiness and positive progress.

6

*Astrology
and
Men*

The most important information that I needed to know was in the stars. But rather than focusing on them, the dark sky had my attention. I did not want to believe in the behavioral characteristics associated with his sign. If I could have just kept an open mind to what was already forecasted, then maybe I could have been saved from heartache. These things, I thought, were not beyond my control. Somehow I felt that I could influence him to act a certain way once he loved me. I soon came to realize that people are the way they are because nature compels them to be that way. More often than not, there is no negotiating with nature.

Very recently I have become fascinated with the stars and the role they play in helping shape an individual's personality traits. The stars only provide a surface look into a person's character; there are many other elements that affect the accuracy of information they provide. A person's name, life path number, and home environment can interfere with astrological information, greatly influencing how an individual acts. Personalized birth charts, which include the person's time and date of birth, are used to provide a much more detailed and accurate picture of an individual. Numerology, specifically in terms of the birth, expression, soul urge, nature, and life path or destiny numbers, provides a very accurate description of an individual's life potential and inherent qualities in contrast to astrology.

The underlying purpose of this section is to not only provide a brief summary of behavioral traits for men according to their sign but to encourage further investigation. By doing this ahead of time, a woman will be more aware and may choose to avoid a serious relationship with the man in question. If there is still a desire to do so, at least she will have an accurate idea of what to expect from his behavior. By taking a scholarly approach to relationships, this will save time and energy. On the one hand, the ability to experience is excellent. On the other, life is too short and too precious to waste time.

The following only provides a general summary of a man's personality traits.

Capricorn: This male is known for being a calm and disciplined individual. He is very motivated to pursue his goals. In relationships, he uses caution before entering a relationship. However, as an earth sign with a strong emotional nature, once he is committed there is the possibility of strong emotional attachment and obsession with his partner. He is the type of man who most likely takes commitments very seriously. He is a loyal, dedicated, and devoted partner. He also may tend to care for the needs of his partner like a father figure.

Aquarius: This man is often not the dating type. Marriage is usually not of high importance either. However, once involved, instead of the average dinner and a movie, this Aquarian man will usually prefer to go to a woman's house for long conversations and sleepovers. He has an odd and unique personality. He prides himself on being that type of guy. Usually generous when it comes to himself, he has a tendency to be selfish and cheap with others.

Pisces: Alcohol, music, and strong-willed women are most likely very appealing to this male. In relationships, he is usually not one for making decisions and will be open to do whatever the woman pleases. Although he is somewhat laid-back, he has a very romantic side and loves to care for the woman in his life. Along with his romantic nature, he is often naturally creative and desires to please his woman in every way. Likewise, he can always be counted upon to be supportive of his partner and her endeavors.

Aries: This man is usually very exciting and never dull. He will most likely be very familiar with romance and know how to be romantic once in a relationship. Although full of ambition and very hardworking, he is usually hard to please. He likes to be waited on hand and foot and is prone to be very bossy. This man feels the need to be agreed with, disliking any criticism. Therefore, he expects his partner to have a "go along with the flow" type of attitude.

Taurus: This man is often known for his ability to be persistent, kind, charming, and seductive. But he can also be stubborn. He thinks highly of material things and is usually willing to put in the effort it takes to attain them. Paranoia is common with this sign. He may have a constant watchful eye for anything suspicious, exhibiting caution when being placed in new situations and around new people. Emotionally, he is not known to be passionate. However, he does possess a depth of feeling that he is not too keen on sharing.

Gemini: He has charisma and definitely knows how to use it. He is most likely highly attracted to the opposite sex, as well as attractive to women. This man may have a reputation as a womanizer because he fails to take relationships or commitments seriously. He also has a tendency to tell lies here and there for his advantage. As a mutable sign, he will be quite the intellectual and conversationalist. Although witty and intelligent, his sign is one that lingers in the air. So proceed with caution, because as soon as he arrives he may likely depart even faster.

Cancer: Cancer is known as the sign of femininity. Therefore, any man born under this sign will have an emotional nature that is more intense than the average. This male is often known for his sensitivity and moodiness. He also has an overbearing personality, which is very likely to exhibit itself in a father-figure or protective role with his partner. Although considered a one-woman type of man, he is somewhat frightened of being in a serious relationship and seeks to avoid them.

Leo: Loyalty is the dominant quality for this man in relationships. However, there is often a huge price to pay for his loyalty. More likely than not, he will expect his partner to worship him. Although his nature is naturally happy and warmhearted, he does have a reputation for being stubborn, hypocritical, and jealous. He feels the need to be the best in everything, making him a fierce competitor. This man tends to have a bullying nature and demands what he wants. With a reputation for manipulation, he encourages others to think and act as he does.

Virgo: This man is known to be very conservative. Obsessed with perfection, he tends to discriminate against things that do not measure up to his standards. Intellectually oriented, he will love information and conversation. He has very strong moral and ethical beliefs that he will have difficulty compromising. Although it usually takes time for him to find a partner who he can give complete devotion to, once involved, he will most likely be warm, loving, and devoted to making the partnership work.

Libra: He has great charm and is usually quite attractive to females. This is due in part to him being in touch with his feminine side. Because he is quite the ladies' man and has most likely had much practice with them, he is a very experienced and suave lover. Due to his idealistic nature, he will always be searching for his idea of the perfect mate. Once in a relationship, he will try his best to avoid any arguments because he is not one for quarrels.

Scorpio: The Scorpio man has a very intense personality. As a fire sign, passion and sex will often be high on his list of likes. This man is not interested in just any sex. His interest lies in great intimacy. Unable to control anger, he is known for having quite a temper. On the bright side, he is often full of determination and has the capacity to succeed. His sarcasm can sometimes be cruel, so if a woman wishes to have a relationship with this man, her skin must not be too thin. Once committed in a relationship, however, this man is often very dedicated and devoted to his mate.

Sagittarius: This male is very active, both in and out of the bedroom. He will be at parties, the movies, or any other place where he can demand attention from people. This male is known for being enthusiastic, curious, and trusting. When there is love in the air, he will be direct and honest with his partner. He is easily attracted to pretty women and falls in love very quickly. He is also likely to have a reputation for being promiscuous. This man most likely doesn't favor longtime commitments, so he will probably have an allergic reaction to the word marriage.

7

One Thing
or
Two
about the
No-Good Man

The following takes a look inside of the mind of a no-good man.

"She doesn't mean anything to me. I say that I love her but don't even make one attempt to look into her eyes when I do. I tell her that she's number one in my life and that's because there's a number two, three, and four. Monogamy doesn't mean shit to me and it never will. There were more women before her and there will be more women after her. She's never met my family. She has never even spoken to my mother. So how could she possibly believe that she is my only lover? I've given her every excuse in the book. 'Baby, I had to work late.' And even when I came home after supposedly being at the office for nearly ten hours and smelled like perfume, I told her that I had gone to the department store to try on some perfume that she would like. And of course she believed me. Damn, sometimes I feel that the S in some women's degrees, BS, stands for stupidity. How could someone believe shit like that?

"I can remember the first time I raised my hand to her. She looked up at me, rolled her eyes then said, 'Baby, I'm sorry for everything I did to make you want to hit me.' After speaking with her family members, she threatened to leave me. 'I'm leaving you!' she yelled. I laughed and called her bluff, and lo and behold, I was right on point. She stayed, providing me with yet another opportunity to slap the shit out of her. How could she have possibly believed that I would change? Yes, I did swear to her on the Lord's Bible. But of course I had my fingers crossed. I even looked her dead in the eyes, with sincerity in my voice and told her that I would never do anything again to hurt her. I swore up and down that I would never do anything to make her suffer emotionally and physically. 'I promise you,' I said. But of course I was always known for my acting ability. Even my friends tell me how much I deserve an Oscar for lying to these bitches. I smile inside every time I think of that when I give her one of my excuses.

"God, I pray. I am so thankful for the women who put up with this nonsense. I am thankful in so many ways for the women who tolerate my ways. Oh yeah, she isn't the first. She is one of many who I have given my sob story to. Please God, don't you ever take these women away. Don't ever take away those who are willing to tolerate my ways, feel sorry enough for me to give me a place to lie in their home and just live, sleep, and shit while I am in between jobs and have nothing to contribute to the household. Please God, don't take away the women who are willing to give me everything, their loving, their uterus, and vagina without protection as I infect them with every disease known to man. Please don't take away their assets, I mean stocks, bonds, money, and that sweet manufactured beehive honey, just for my long john silver. Please God or Jesus Christ, whoever may be listening, if you just do me that favor and allow for that species of women to continue, I'll be the best no-good man that I can possibly be. I promise. But this time my fingers are not crossed."

Like an eclipse, the good man is a rare phenomenon. On the contrary, his evil twin is as prevalent as unpurified H_2O. The no-good man cannot be deduced down to a specific structure because he comes in all sizes, shades, astrological signs, nationalities, and faiths. He speaks every language imaginable, from English to Enga. He is a lawyer, doctor, entertainer, or cashier. The no-good man pandemic is everywhere. He is at the grocery store, a child's school, sitting in the subway station, college class, or in his car waiting for the red light to turn green. Unlike a drug test, there is no radar or device that allows for a woman to automatically detect what type of man he is. This often results in involvement, then heartache.

The no-good man is pollution with a penis. Like environmental pollutants, he seeks to disrupt and taint the atmosphere of a woman with his negativity. For the no-good man does not love. He only lusts for what a woman can provide him with: sex, money, and all of the other things that money can buy. He is a worthless specimen with the DNA of a dog that loves and lives for tapping into a woman's weakness. For within this weakness there is a well with an abundance of water ready to pour out all she has to offer to keep him satisfied. This is sometimes her remedy for repairing wounds that have forever haunted her life.

Women must not be mistaken. The art of grave digging did not die when the last Egyptian tomb was raided thousands of years ago. In fact, the no-good man continues this legacy by being a modern-day grave digger. Like the ancients, he knows the location of the gold and jewels. What is worthwhile is worthy of his effort. He knows that what a woman possesses is worthwhile in every aspect. This is why he targets the woman and is willing to go to a great extent to capture her jewels. In most cases, the level of professionalism applied is equivalent to years and years of intense training.

Frequently, the no-good man will use commitment as a smoke screen. Many no-good men hide behind a wedding band, which fails to transform a no-good man into a good one. The no-good man may be well-endowed physically and financially stable. Sexually, he may be able to please with 999 ways to interact his pole with a hole. Initially, the no-good man may be very generous with what he has to offer, including compliments and gifts. Frequently, it is this abundance of generosity that allows a woman to fall in love with him and mistake the infatuation for what he can provide superficially for love. But this is a disguise. The materials and his gift to sexually please are all tactics of his magician's act. They cover up his lack of truth and respect. These things are used to draw the woman into his game, diverting her attention away from the deceit. The no-good man uses this to make a woman tolerate his nonsense and stay. For the man is very aware of the woman's emotional nature. He is aware that once emotionally committed and attached, there will be a high level of devotion, commitment, and forgiveness.

In the beginning, the veteran will disguise himself as a gentleman by opening doors and saying thank-you. He will be interested in everything a woman has to say, giving the impression he is actually listening. The veteran's game and verbally persuasive words will be superb, tight, and together like his name is Milton Bradley. This man will be like a chameleon with the ability to blend into any environment or situation perfectly and tell the woman what she has always been waiting to hear at the exact time she wants to hear it. Unfortunately, his bite will be like a scorpion's, debilitating and hypnotic, persuading the woman to believe and do as he says.

As time goes by, some no-good men become easily detectable. Either these men will have a certain reputation or they will have certain playboy mannerisms, such as never returning phone calls or being only interested in sexual relations. On the other hand, some no-good men can be in the beginning stages of no-goodness. It is quite possible that they will still have some humanity and decency within themselves that encourage honesty about commitment and where a woman stands in their life. On the contrary, the no-good specialists or veterans are those who perfect the art of manipulation by giving the appearance of being genuine and legitimate. These players know how to use deceit and lies as their means of capturing the woman's heart, using it to their advantage.

The no-good man is known for his excuses. In fact, it is his forte. He will have excuses for every day of the year and even an extra one for a leap year. The no-good man loves excuses because they relieve him of the responsibility to be a real man.

Excuse #1: "Oh honey, I'm a sex addict. And you're always working. If you can't give it to me, then I have to get it from somewhere else."

Response: "Oh really. Is there an actual clinical diagnosis for this? Let me see your doctor's signature on the diagnosis card. You are not man enough to keep it in your pants, and now it is some overwhelming condition. You need to sell those beans to another Jack-in-the-stalk, jackass."

Excuse #2: "Baby, I didn't answer my phone because my battery only had one bar. It actually died right in the middle of the phone ringing."

Response: "Don't give me that nonsense! These damn phone batteries are like Energizer bunnies. They keep going and going and going. And for your information, I sure would prefer that bunny hop on me because even the Lord knows that after the second hop you're done. But you know what, from now on you can take your Motorola and talk to your Hotorola all you wish."

Excuse #3: "That lipstick mark close to my mouth is from my mother."

Response: "I don't know what type of incest nonsense that's going on in your family but that is not legal in New York."

Excuse #4: "I only smell like fish because a couple of friends and I ate at a fish market today."

Response: "Okay, red snapper! Things are about to get really red up in here. And I bet you can't find this swimming in the bottom of the Atlantic."

Excuse #5: "We don't have to do anything spectacular. Let me just introduce you to my vernacular. Let's chill!"

Response: "What? This isn't 1987, and I'm not a member of Guy! If you don't have any money, then don't expect any of my honey!"

Lies are the no-good man's oxygen. He lives off lies and like any person on life support, once the oxygen is taken away, he will die. Lies allow him to disguise himself as a good man. Lies allow for the no-good man to make progress with a woman. He will say, "Baby, you are the only one." The phone calls will then stop for a week. Like nothing has happened, he will reappear. He will say, "Baby, I love you," and then call that same woman a bitch one hour later. He will say, "Baby, you are the light of my life," but in his mind, he is just referring to the matches that he uses for his cigarettes. He will say, "I want to marry you." But he will never actually propose and never plan on doing so. Or sometimes the reverse will occur. He will actually marry the woman but still continue on in his ways.

He will apologize with those puppy dog eyes a million and one times for all he has done to hurt the woman in his life. Magically and more often than not, a woman will forgive the wrongdoing. But the same mistakes and apologies will never end. Love will allow a woman to forget the main purpose of an apology, which is to not allow the same mistake to happen again. If this happens, then what was the purpose of that apology? If there is any confusion, then allow me to clarify. It is to keep her mind tolerant. It is to keep her in the relationship. It is to keep her hopes for better and brighter days more optimistic than ever. It is a part of the ploy of **man**ipulation. This will keep the relationship at a relationship level so that it will never elevate into a realationship.

The departure of fiction and confrontation of reality is inevitable. Indeed, one day a woman may finally take a stand and threaten him with the words, "I'm leaving you." If the woman has not yet acted on this threat, then she must come to acknowledge that every time she supplies him with those infamous words, "I'm leaving you," he will see through her thoughts, phrases, and intentions like her mind is transparent. The no-good man is fully aware that when a woman threatens him with abandoning her love and support that she is trying to make his heart full of fear. In fact, the woman seems to be forgetting a major fact. The no-good man knows exactly her motives and what she wants out of him.

In terms of the no-good man and the company that he keeps, always remember that birds of a feather flock together. In the wild, we will never see tigers hanging around giraffes unless they are about to be recycled. Thus, no-good men are usually friends with other no-good men because dogs of a kennel share, not only friendship, but kinship as well. They actually prefer this type of company because it gives them a way to compare and contrast the results of each other's behavior to figure out who has more game. The one who is most successful will feel a greater sense of manhood by knowing that he is better at his game than his competitors.

The no-good man avoids the strong-minded woman at all costs. Why? The no-good man considers the strong-minded woman as too much of a challenge because he prefers the easy route. For a strong-minded woman has a concrete barrier, making the mind very difficult to infiltrate and manipulate. It is this independent woman who threatens the very existence of the no-good man. This woman has set high standards and expectations for herself and her partner and can most likely see through the cheap cologne, glitzy speech, and cunning tactics.

Who is the main prey of the no-good man?

The no-good man prefers interacting with women who have already been emotionally and physically broken down so he will not have much work to do.

A Woman with Dependencies: Dependencies = Anesthesia. They allow us to cope with what we feel is lacking, but they do not heal us. They discreetly harm the body by allowing us to neglect the real issues, keeping them alive and well. Whether there is an attachment to sex, materials, food, etc., they all numb the body from pain and replace it with false feelings of happiness. In the mind of the dependent, these artificial preservatives increase the feeling of self-worth that are naturally absent.

Physical or Emotional Insecurities: Those who carry internal pollution are more apt to accept external pollution. They will also be less reluctant to exude confidence.

A Victim of Emotional or Physical Abuse: This is from either a familial or romantic standpoint. This increases a woman's ability to tolerate the continuation of such behavior from others. Being that the mental state is in a diminished capacity, this allows for continued victimization. This also makes a woman complacent with mediocrity.

Younger or Underage: A girl has less mental development than a woman. This increases her ability to be influenced and led astray by those who have more experience with life and relationships.

Grew Up Without a Father Figure or a Positive Male Role Model: This type of woman may be looking for someone to fill that void of fatherly love. Not having an accurate representation of what a good man is supposed to be, she will eagerly accept and tolerate compliments, support, and all other things not experienced in early childhood. The acceptance of nonsense will be right behind.

A Female Who Has Been the Victim of Rape Or Sexual Abuse: This woman may view herself as recycled material: picked up when needed, used and abused, thrown away, then picked up again for the same purpose. Thus, recycled material will have a recycled mentality. Since it has already happened once, then it will happen again without the woman questioning the pattern or seeking to stop it. This female is also more likely to become involved in exploitative occupations such as prostitution, the porn industry, stripping, being a X-rated video whore, or any other related field.

Unaccustomed to the Finer Things in Life: This woman may have come from impoverished surroundings. She may have had some hardships, emotional and/or physical. When a woman is not accustomed to luxury, she will more likely be complacent with a man's mediocrity.

A Woman Who Dresses in a Trashy Manner: A decent man is attracted to a decent woman. A good man is attracted to a woman who conceals her precious jewels. The only thing a woman dressed like a slut will attract is a stray dog.

Regardless of which category a woman falls into, the no-good man will still seek to target and manipulate that weakness in order to control the situation.

Exploring the existence of the no-good man brings me to the first question. Who is responsible for the no-good man? The general concept is that the individual is always responsible for their own actions. For it is a voluntary choice whether to be a good person or a bad person. Nonetheless, society does endorse certain behaviors.

Sex is highly ranked on society's list. There is no denying this, for society thrives and progresses from sex. Procreation is a must. Even if there is no sexual interaction, there is still sex. For the very roots of the human are gender and sex, Adam and Eve, or man and woman. Society sells sex through advertising. Even if advertisements ceased to exist, sexuality could still sell itself. Everywhere we go, our eyes come in contact with some form of bodily expression or exploitation, whether in music videos, commercials, advertisements, or just plain human contact.

Many studies suggest that the majority of a man's thoughts revolve around sex. Statistics say that men are prone to think about sex every eighteen seconds. Naturally, men become excited when there is any exposure of the female flesh. Men are also prone to become very weak when sex is a variable in an equation. Since it is believed that the majority of a man's thinking is centered around sex, then it is their ultimate motivation. Advertising executives know that if they want their product to be number one, specifically with men, then they must target the very foundation of a man's weakness by exciting his loins. If they target the very essence of a man's thinking, then they influence his urge to buy a certain product.

In relation to male sexuality, society is responsible for the creation and definition of what constitutes a man by advocating certain "manly" behaviors. For instance, a man is seldom given praise for monogamy. If a man has never been intimate with a female or is not a "ladies' man," his heterosexuality is questioned, resulting in ostracism. Therefore, according to societal standards, it pays to play the field. Thus, when examining the no-good man, we must not neglect how society motivates men to quench their sexual thirst through various tactics. Society will nurture the continuation of the no-good man, furthering their existence. Nonetheless, it is the woman who is unable to say no to him and yes to herself who keeps the no-good man in business.

Sexual exploration is sometimes a tricky subject. As humans, we cannot help but to have urges. If there is no commitment or a consequence, then there is nothing wrong with giving into temptation and exploring a desire. However, it is the no-good man's natural weakness that allows for him to give into this temptation when in a relationship. This exposure will increase the weakness of his already weak mind, completely debilitating the no-good man's mind and allowing for his body to follow into temptation. This will allow the mind to be on one track, de-emphasizing everything else. On the other hand, it is the good man who will not allow such temptation to lead him astray, for his mind is too strong for such a ploy and he will firmly stand his ground.

An important concern includes the question, "Why is the no-good man no-good?" There are countless answers to this question. Each man has his own individual reason for being no-good. He could be trying to compensate for his lack of self-esteem or manliness. There may have been no exposure to positive images during childhood, including inappropriate behavior, disrespect toward women, and a fragmented family structure. Alternative explanations include the possibility of genetic inheritance. But who cares? The more time spent on the no-good man's problems, the less time there is to dedicate and discover a solution to the issues that allow for a woman to tolerate his ways. In other words, let sleeping dogs lie in their own shit.

Many women may wonder if the no-good man will ever change. There are some no-good men who will eventually learn the value of a woman and how to feel with their hearts. There are some that will also come to learn to respect, monogamy, and how to appreciate only one woman. An important thing to note when considering change is that there is no specific way to determine when or if change will actually come because every individual is different.

The most important thing to remember is that no matter the amount of her beauty, intelligence, or the size of a woman's assets, a no-good man will not change unless he first realizes his ways are a problem and seeks to eradicate his behavior. For the majority of no-good men's interest lies in the p, and that does not stand for the first letter in personality. The woman should not be fooled with the belief that she can trick a no-good man into change and commitment with a child. If he does not treat the woman well, then how does she think he is going to treat something that came from her uterus? Last but not least, do not think for a minute that marriage will change the no-good man. The only difference is the involvement of a higher entity with the deceit.

There are various factors that can trigger change. Boredom is one. As living the player lifestyle becomes less exciting, the need to settle down can begin to become a primary concern. When this happens and the whore becomes less appealing, there will be more interest in the wholesome woman. As a result, the no-good man will seek change in his ways. The motivation for change can also come after the loss of a good, loyal, and loving woman, along with the difficulty of discovering another woman of her distinct qualities.

Sometimes to really appreciate and cherish a past love, we must lose it. Just like a good man, a good woman is not the easiest to find. This experience will hopefully open up the eyes, allowing for the body to discover how rare encountering a true and genuine person really is. In the case of the no-good man, he will come to realize how a good woman is the backbone of a man's foundation, be remorseful for his past actions, and be better to the next woman who comes along. However, we must realize that this change is voluntary and has to come as a result of his own individual will and desire. No human can be coerced into anything that there is no natural feeling to do. No one will change just for the sake of another's conscience.

Very cleverly, the no-good man will have a magnificent way of concealing who he truly is. But lies do not linger for too long. Once given the chance, his true colors will be revealed like a rainbow after a storm, introducing the woman to this grown boy disguised as a man.

8

The No-Good Woman

The following reflects the thoughts of the no-good woman.

"In God we trust, but in deceit I lust. You see, my purpose upon this earth is rooted in evil. When it comes to men, I do not love. I cannot love. Let me clarify, oh how I do love the green that comes from within their pockets. I crave this green and will lie to any extent, resort to any means to get it from him. I will cheat, steal, and do all and anything within the power of my bones to supply myself with those dead trees. I will lie on my back, get on my knees, and beg please just to get a taste of what will satisfy my cravings. But it's all good because I feel as though I have no mind and nothing more to offer than what lies between the crevices of my thighs.

"Don't even think if you have a man with monetary means that I won't grab him. What you can do I can do ten times better with enthusiasm that will create a memorable orgasm. Please don't think that what you have is gold, and he is only sold to you. I will borrow him when need be and when I'm done, don't worry, I'll give him back to you with a disease. You see, I have no morals and ethics. I use and abuse, not caring about the hearts I confuse. I will always be a no-good woman until I *fully understand and am a recipient of the damage that I cause. But until that day arrives, I will keep using his wet towel to my advantage until it's dry. Now this will create a cavity, not only in my mouth but in between my thighs. I will be used and abused, not for my intellect but my tools. But if it is for legal tender, I will never mind being turned into a fool."*

That's right! Being no-good does not discriminate. It is an equal opportunity employer. To mention the no-good man without mentioning the no-good woman would be an incomplete portrayal of the no-good population. Yes, this book is solely dedicated to the plight of the woman and her interaction with the no-good man. However, much needs to be said about the no-good woman who can threaten how a man views and conceptualizes what a woman should represent: a respectable female who carries herself in the highest esteem. A woman who carries herself in the opposite regard will be abandoned and regarded by men who have had their hearts tarnished by her deceitful ways as a slut or bitch.

The interaction between the good man and the no-good woman will sometimes persuade a man's view of women, in general, to be heartless and ruthless. This thought can then motivate him to be vengeful and spiteful toward other future prospects. Now am I saying that the no-good woman is responsible for turning good men into no-good men? No, I am not suggesting that his presence is solely due to her, but it could be a possible explanation, along with other factors, that contributes to the no-good man's mental state and behavior.

The no-good woman is dependent. Her survival is based upon the support that others give her. She will definitely carry dirt under her fingernails, especially when she has just finished with their primary job of gold digging. For there is no denying that some no-good women walk around with so much dirt underneath their fingernails that they could be easily mistaken for construction workers. In fact, their primary prey is often men in committed relationships; this sometimes includes marriage. The no-good woman loves the thought of taking another woman's man. This may make her feel like she is more of a woman because she was able to intercept the effort another woman has put into a relationship and scoop him up. "Yes, your man chose me over you," is what she says with a smile.

Honesty is not a quality of her character. She is manipulative and uses lies to receive benefits from others. A common tactic of the no-good woman may be to trick a guy into pregnancy, allowing for her and the child to depend on what he has to offer. The no-good woman utilizes her physical attributes and gifts of persuasion to manipulate her prey. Just like her male twin, once emotional attachment has been achieved, she goes in for the attack. She will tell this man, "Baby, you are the only one." But the actual truth will be that this man is the fourth person she has said that to in the week. As the no-good woman does not embrace commitment or fidelity, she will often have more than one relationship at a time.

The financial portfolio of the no-good woman is not defined in terms of stocks, but cocks. Her weapon of choice is not the mind with its ability to think and promote individual growth; it is sex. She is aware that when it comes to sex, the majority of men will go to a great extent to fulfill their sexual desire and keep it satisfied. Therefore, she will use her ability to sexually please to exploit the whims and weaknesses of a man. In return, she expects for that man to provide her with what she wants. She is not interested in loving or providing a man with emotional support. Her very existence is rooted in a pursuit of self-satisfaction and progression first, second, and last.

The no-good woman can sometimes be found shaking that ass for cash. She may even be found twirling around a silver pole for some gold. That's right! The name of this woman's game is laziness.

She doesn't want to go out and make her own money the honest and right way but finds other ways. Instead of using her mind to exercise power, she uses her sexual power to get what she wants from men. As a result, the no-good woman may either have multiple baby fathers, one, or none. There can also be lingering paternity tests for her children. Unfortunately, even after becoming a biological mother, the definition of mother can still remain an undeserved title. For after birth, her sole pursuit may still be to satisfy herself first, allowing the neglect of her child.

The idea that every woman deserves a good man is a misconception. The only woman who deserves a good man is a good woman. Only these two can form the basis of not a relationship, but a realationship. As in algebra, a negative multiplied by a negative equals a positive. If a no-good man initiates a relationship with a no-good woman, or vice versa, this will equate in a positive relationship. The no-good woman and the no-good man are equally deserving of one another because when paired together they create a platform where both parties combine with one another to equal out the negativity that exists individually. Thus, they will each get what they are worthy of, nonsense.

In terms of the no-good woman, fate will soon take its course. The common saying, "What goes around comes around," is applicable. Those women who have hurt many hearts in their days will definitely feel that pain. As a general rule, she must meet her match and encounter an individual who toys around with emotions. Once this occurs, the no-good woman will realize that life is not like a merry-go-round. For it is merry, when it goes around, but to the person who had to catch that negative ball, it will not be a merry experience. And just as the merry-go-round goes around, when it comes back around and the person who threw that ball has to catch it with their own glove, it will prove to be not so merry after all.

Much time needs to be spent addressing the no-good woman and the no-good man who hold the future of the youth in the palms of their hands and continue to misrepresent the true definition of a man and a woman. As they are the current and future role models, it is a sad day in the land of motherhood and fatherhood when one or the other is in charge of a child's upbringing. The power they possess will influence and shape the fate of their child's relationship with the opposite sex. A lack of proper care can result in a new generation of no-good men and women. This ultimately sets up what a child will or will not tolerate from the opposite sex.

A child's definition of strength and respect, not only for themselves but for others, is not received from *Webster's Dictionary* but from the images they see and the people with whom they interact on a constant basis. The lack or abundance of strength the parent has is reflected in their child. A parent can preach all they want, but if this is not followed by practice then the preaching has no value. If a mother wishes to have a strong daughter, then she must be a strong mother. If a mother wants to have a strong son, then she must be a strong mother. If a father wants to have a strong daughter, then he must be a strong father. If a father wishes to have a strong son, then he must be a strong father.

It is true. The children have important choices to make now and once they become adults later. Whether a child chooses to become involved in an emotionally or physically abusive relationship, as either the abuser or the abused, is greatly motivated and influenced by a generational cycle. On many occasions, children have witnessed abuse happening to their mothers or seen this behavior by their fathers and begin to inherit these traits as the appropriate way to conduct a relationship. Therefore, parental power must be handled cautiously.

There is no denying that both the no-good females and no-good males are increasing at an alarming rate. Which prevails more, the no-good man or the no-good woman? There are more women who suffer from the emotional abuses of men than vice versa. There are more women who suffer from domestic violence than men. There are more single mothers raising children than single fathers. There is also a larger percentage of fathers who don't have a role in their child's life. This evidence supports the theory that the no-good man is more prevalent than the no-good woman.

If this section adequately describes you and your interaction with men, then I encourage you to take a stand. I encourage you to take a deep and long look into the mirror and really analyze what you see. Ask yourself if this is the way you wish to continue to represent yourself. I encourage you to examine your path. Your current route is destined for destruction. A real woman does not use and abuse hearts for her sole benefit. A real woman does not carry herself like a cubic zirconium but like a diamond. A real woman stands on her own two feet and uses her potential to succeed. I encourage you to embrace that real woman who lies within. Cease allowing that girl who represents you to plague and disrupt the very nature and essence of your womanhood.

9

Words of Wisdom
2
the Woman
in His Life

What is it about this man? Is it the way the blood trickles down your face and neck? What motivates you to stay? Is it because there is the hope of some day meeting his mother and father, although it has already been more than one year? Or is it the way he steals from the same purse that you use to support your children?

Is it because you have convinced yourself that his "goods" are made out of gold? Is that the main reason why you continue to sell the Devil your soul? Or is it the orgasms he makes you have? Is it because you look in the mirror and believe that the image reflected back upon you is not good enough to have someone treat you with respect? Is it the way he calls you? "Bitch, come here." Is it the intonation of his voice? Is it how his mouth closes after he has insulted the very essence of your womanhood? Is it because of his "good" hair, "pretty" eyes, or "nice" skin complexion that you so desperately wish your child to have, the reason why you still tolerate his ways? Is it the way he tells you that he loves you right after you've found phone numbers of other women in his pocket?

Is how he looks at other females while you two are together the reason why you still consider him to be the one you've always wished for? Is it how he cheats on you with so many different women that you've lost count? Or could it happen to be that his smacks compensate for the void of not being loved by your father? Does that fill the emptiness of your mother never giving you those hugs and words of encouragement that you really needed when you were feeling your worst? What urges you to continue? What's the reason you can love a man who does everything wrong? What endures your heart, mind, body, and soul to stay in such an emotionally, physically, and mentally destructive relationship? Are these questions so real that they urge you to close the cover of this book and never pick it up again?

A Good Woman + A No-good man = Destruction
A Strong Woman + A Weak Man = Destruction
A Good Woman - A No-good Man = Success
A Strong Woman - A Weak Man = Success

The no-good man is not therapy. He is destruction. The no-good man is not a quick-fix solution that will solve a woman's problems. He will only add to them. The no-good man will not cure the pain from the abandonment of a father. The no-good man will not cure the emotional neglect of a woman's mother. The no-good man cannot compensate for a woman's lack of self-love. Only the woman can solve what lingers within. For the no-good man can only bring the woman down, not build her up.

Everything that a woman needs to achieve she was equipped with at birth: mind, body, soul, and spirit. The ability to be a woman does not mean that more focus needs to go into the last three letters of the title *woman*, neglecting the word as a whole. A woman should not seek to make the last three letters a first priority. Giving focus to the entire five letters must always be her first priority.

Before a woman can learn to love someone else, she must first learn to love herself. The love of self, the ability to cherish and behold the beauty of self, the ability to define self and stand alone as an individual who only relies upon herself, is the solution. Ultimately, there are only two people a woman needs to succeed. The first person is God. The second person's name not only begins with an M, but this M also indicates the first letter of the device that allows for us to physically recognize the answer. No, it is not a man. For a woman does not need a penis to progress. It is a mirror that allows a woman to see *me*.

A woman will often allow herself to be mistreated when she feels worthless. When we think little of ourselves, then we lower our standards and accept negativity. This feeling of a lowered self-worth sends us treasure hunting in the wrong locations. It is the inner issues that keep us from embracing ourselves as the diamonds we are. It is the pollution on the inside that makes us absorb the pollution on the outside, allowing for that no-good man to treat us like a cubic zirconium. We will then find excuses to justify this behavior.

In order to build a good partnership, its foundation must involve two good or positive participants. As in algebra, a negative times a positive equals a negative. A negative plus a positive equals the sign of whichever number is larger. Therefore, regardless of the quantity of the negative number, its negativity still decreases the sum. In a relationship, if one party is positive or good and the other is negative or no-good, this will diminish the potential of the relationship's ability to be beneficial to both parties. Ultimately, "AAD," is the phrase that pays: Acknowledge, Act, Depart. For a woman to subtract the no-good man from her life, she must first add all the signs together to find that subtraction of the man is necessary.

The key fact that a woman must realize when interacting with a man is that he will only do to her what she allows him to. Although a woman may continuously warn and threaten him with those infamous words, "I'm leaving you," words have no weight without action. When a woman accepts the no-good man's nonsense, she helps him succeed as a no-good man. This allows for the no-good man to become a professional in his field. Once the woman realizes, acknowledges, and accepts who she is dealing with, the second step is to acquire strength; the third is to take action. When reading this, some may cringe at the notion of being strong enough to say no to the no-good man she loves. But within every woman lies strength. The only difficulty that this presents is finding its location.

Men may control the world, but women control its gold mines. Not to be confused with bronze, the metal that lies within these mines are gold. However, some women really do treat it like a metal of lesser value. We must realize that what lies in between our thighs is a golden and powerful asset. We must learn to properly exercise this power. If every woman would exercise the right to use the padlock and restrict access, a change would be right around the corner. If a child's toys and privileges are taken away, their behavior changes. Or better yet, do not grant the privilege in the first place until his behavior proves him worthy of having it.

When in search of that perfect man, a woman should approach the dating arena just as an athlete would approach the Olympics. That's right! A woman should always compete for the gold. Unfortunately, some women seem to be content with competing for the bronze. Just because a woman has "man" in her title does not mean that she must be the man and woman within the relationship. For a woman should never have to fill in for him because of his irresponsibility. A relationship is deserving of one hundred percent on both sides. Settling for a bronze gives her not a man but a boy disguised as one.

The no-good men who portray themselves to be gold on the outside are the human dogs of society. However, once interacting with these men, they will reveal what they are, fools' gold, by responding to responsibility negatively. But why should a woman have to deal with a dog? For a dog is only good for fetching slippers and performing tricks. Remember, a dog is a man's best friend, not a woman's. Why else do dog and men bond so easily? The answer happens to be very simple. They share a hereditary linking. Thus, a woman should never feel as though she has an obligation to a man who has voluntarily chosen to take on the behavioral traits of his canine comrade.

Present-day society rewards women with options. A woman does not have to tolerate the humanized dog. A woman should access her right to release him to the proper authorities. The number of non-profit companies that adopt and nurture dogs is amazingly high. From the ASPCA to the North Shore Animal League, there are various organizations committed to relieving the heavy burdens that dogs create in society. Realistically, the only difficulty this presents is providing a cage large enough to fit the specific stray dog. If he is as "cute" as believed, then he should have no problem getting adopted.

Much time needs to be spent addressing the woman who seeks out the no-good man because she is attracted to the idea of spontaneity. She wants a thrill. She desires some excitement and a challenge in her life. If she seeks this, she must also take full responsibility for the emotional consequences of being involved with a man who has already, by the choices he has made, demonstrated that he has little to no care about the quality of his own life. Thus, how can she expect him to have any concern for hers?

Some women know prior to walking in the specific path that shit is right around the corner. However, they still proceed in that same direction because they are in love with taking a risk. Perhaps it is the thrill of the ride. But a woman should keep in mind that roller coasters can give upset stomachs too. Sometimes it is the excitement of having a man who has a reputation or a man who is known to be disrespectful. For a woman can be convinced that she is related to the great Houdini, having in her loins the magic ability to convert him into a faithful and respectable man. And to all those women who insist upon fighting over the no-good man, please take heed. Only flies are supposed to fight over shit.

Oftentimes, she is attracted to knowing a man has the potential of controlling her life, controlling what she does and says. It could be the thought of knowing that he lives the life of an outlaw, on the edge or suspected to be involved with numerous women to whom he has done the same nonsense. Sometimes it is the thought of this man having a reputation with other women who have had to put him out along with the morning's garbage that adds a feeling of excitement. A woman must bear in mind that one woman's trash is not another woman's treasure. The same garbage that stunk up one woman's house will do the same in another woman's home. The trash is on the corner for a reason. If he has done this before with someone else, more likely than not his behavior will continue. So a woman should not be so eager to rush out and recycle the trash before the sanitation department has arrived. How can we ever expect to rid the trash if we continue to recycle it?

There is no denying that love is a beautiful and amazing emotion. But a woman should not allow love to make a fool out of her. Consider this question, how can a no-good man define a woman's worth when he is worthless? Everyone wants and needs love but everyone is not deserving of it or capable of adequately displaying it. Although it is true that no human being is perfect, a woman's ultimate goal should be to find a man with the least amount of flaws. However, if the man's true colors begin to show, then a woman has a responsibility to herself to say yes to her internal strength by saying no to the external weakness disguised as the no-good man.

If a woman happens to believe she has yet to encounter a no-good man, rest assured, he will arrive. It may not be today, tomorrow, or eight weeks from now, but when her world is disrupted by his presence, it will be shocking. When interacting with a man whom a woman has yet to accept as being no-good, nine times out of ten, if she has an instinct or suspects any signs of infidelity, then her suspicion is most likely correct. Remember that wise saying, "Never change the first answer that enters into your head because it is usually the correct one."

Ultimately, there comes a time when a woman has to stop listening to the no-good man and use her own mind to come to the truth. One must listen and come to a decision with the eyes, not with the ears, and certainly not with the heart. A woman must wake up and smell the coffee. A woman must not only drink it but also digest it. I want the black words from this book to be that black coffee. Do not just read them; digest them. Use and apply them to the situation at hand. Thus the eyes will be revitalized with 20/20 vision and come to see that when you look at yourself as fool's gold, you allow for any fool to have access.

10

The Possible Effects of Being Involved with a No-Good Man

Lowered self-esteem

Depression

Possible exposure to HIV and other STDs

Missing out on the opportunity to be with a good man

Destroyed peace of mind

Sharing a child with an unfit father

If children witness this type of behavior, they become prone to exhibit or tolerate it in later years.

Being prone to gossip and ridicule by others who know what's going on

Lack of motivation, confidence, strength, and the overall ability to think for one's self because the situation creates a tendency to believe and accept everything. As a result, the mind becomes relaxed from the lack of exercising its ability to think and can become complacent and not think at all.

The longer the situation, the more it enables the ability to tolerate, not only the present no-good man, but the others who linger and await in the future.

Isolation and separation from family, friends, and others who seek to help and uplift the woman

And worst of all, a battered, bruised, and broken heart

11

What a True Good Man Is All About

He will be emotionally, physically, and financially stable or at least striving to be.

He will never lift a finger to hit his woman because, even if he has the urge to, his respect for women outweighs that urge.

He will always be honest and open in his communication.

He will never complain, rush, or make his woman feel guilty if she wants to wait before intimacy.

He will keep his woman's secrets close to his heart and never share them with anyone else.

He will be able to compromise.

He will always remember anniversaries, special occasions, and moments that have meaning to his woman and the relationship.

He will always be there for her, emotionally and physically.

He will always respect his woman inside and outside the home and will never call her any other name besides endearing terms.

He will take care of his responsibility inside and outside of the relationship.

He will always hold the door for his woman in public, and pull her seat out before sitting in a restaurant, or at least give the gesture of being a gentleman.

He will be cordial to her mother and any other female member in her family.

He will always be compassionate, understanding, and considerate of his woman's feelings and needs.

He will provide his woman with motivation and encouragement to succeed with her goals.

He will never try to control his woman's actions or thoughts, and he will let her be who she is and never try to change her.

What type of woman does a good man want?

A good man wants a good woman. Specifically, a good man wants a woman who he will be honored to take home and introduce to his parents, family, and friends. Class is something that she possesses. This woman will have a high level of self-awareness. She will be independent and stand on her own two feet. This woman will be headed in a positive direction in life. She will be confident enough to recognize her potential to succeed, yet down-to-earth enough to not be filled with conceit. Ultimately, this is the same type of woman a no-good man may prefer, but it is the good man who will do right by this woman.

12

Warning Signs

While learning basic mathematics, we are taught how to add numbers together in order to receive a certain answer. And just like math, we all have the ability to retrieve a certain answer from certain actions, otherwise known as warning signs.

A man who can provide no positive and long-term benefits is a no-good man. The identification of a no-good man is not limited to his romantic interaction with the woman in his life. It also includes his response to responsibilities in general, his direction and path in life, and how he interacts with others. Thus, I advise every woman to pay very close attention to the following words. For within these pages are the most obvious, or sometimes not so obvious, warning signs that reveal what type of man a woman is really involved with. And be aware, when this behavior happens once, it will happen twice and occur continuously until all ties are severed. If the leash fits, then let that dog wear it!

He is definitely a no-good man when:

There has ever been physical or verbal abuse. There is *never* a justifiable reason for this type of behavior.

There has ever been a threat of physical harm.

There is no recollection of the last time he had a job because he has every intention of living off of someone.

He has an entire army of baby mommas and drama to go along with those mommas.

He does not physically, emotionally, or financially support his child. Whether he has one child or five, if he only supports four of those children, then he is still a deadbeat.

There have been any instances of theft.

He has any type of addiction and he is not trying to get help for it.

He does not treat his mother with respect. A woman can predict her treatment by observing the manner in which he responds, treats, and interacts with important women in his life, as well as random women he comes into contact with.

He has ever cheated. Here the idea of once a dog, always a dog, comes into play. Provide him with a pink slip and some coupons for Alpo. After you have sent him to the unemployment line, you can continue on with your life.

There has never been a gift for Valentine's Day, Christmas, or a birthday. These holidays are like kryptonite to the no-good man. No one, I repeat, no one is that damn broke.

He complains about this book. The truth can be very hard to digest. Therefore, many no-good men have trouble confronting and accepting this. Hearing something that is not positive and can be directly connected to them causes them to lash out. The only thing a good man has to worry about is a woman looking for 999 ways to tell him yes.

He is constantly doing a magician's disappearing act, whereas the only time he does manage to appear is for a booty call or anything else for his sole benefit.

He may be a no-good man when:

The relationship has been ongoing for more than two years and he has not yet proposed. What is he waiting for, the United States to elect an African-American president? Or perhaps he is just so accustomed to receiving his milk for free that he has no intention upon purchasing the farm and cow. That is just some calcium for thought.

There are rumors about how much of a player he is, or any other type of negative comments. Do not be so eager to label these claims as false; give them some consideration. Remember, third parties can sometimes see a situation more clearly. Do not find fault with the person who is finding fault with the man in question. Although everyone is innocent until proven guilty, one should take into consideration the credibility and reliability of the source.

He has pimp or player with a secondary alias or identity. Take this literally and truthfully. This is a wake-up call.

He is giving an explanation and does not make direct eye contact. This is usually the primary sign that his words are false. Body language will reveal hidden truths that words do not. Sweaty palms, no direct eye contact, and fidgeting are all warning signs of deceit.

He has wandering eyes for other women in public.

He has been dishonest, and you feel as though you cannot trust him. A woman must learn how to trust her instincts. Nine times out of ten it is correct.

There has been no formal introduction to his family or friends as his "girlfriend," although it may be too early to determine if the relationship is serious or this woman is deserving of that title.

There are too many compliments or gifts. This could mean he is suffering from a guilty conscience or just trying to find a way to discover "Victoria's secret." Overdoing the compliments is very suspicious and makes one wonder if the words are truly genuine. In the event of gifts, he could be trying to buy love and affection or undo some wrong action that may either be known or unknown to the recipient.

He does not give out his home phone number or invite the woman to his home. Most likely he is trying to conceal something. He is probably living a double life. He may have a wife or another woman whom he is living with. He could still be living at home with his mother. A man who uses discretion in that manner usually has something to hide.

13

Learning How 2 Say No

Saying yes is so easy but saying no is so hard. I would have preferred writing a fifteen-page research paper for a political science class. I used to wonder what made it so difficult to say "no." I thought if no is one of the most basic words in the English vocabulary, then why was it so difficult for me to say it? If a two-year-old child can say no, then why can't I, an adult, utter those two letters and mean it?

The mind wonders and begins to think. Fear and nervousness slowly creep into the body. Then, to some, the questions may come. How can I say no to the deceit that I've said yes to for so long? How do I walk away from the promises to do better? How do I walk away from, "I'm sorry baby. It'll never happen again?" How do I neglect the look of sympathy and sorrow in his puppy dog eyes as I say no and never again? How do I walk away from "I love you. Don't do this. I'll be a better man?" How do I ignore his words when my heart and body just want to embrace them and love him for the good times that we shared together? How do I just say no and abandon all the time and effort that I have so diligently

placed into making this relationship work? Oh God, give me an answer.
How will I?

After all the "hows" have been said and done, the "nows" and "nos"
can begin by remembering the heartache, the tears, and the infidelity.
That is the only way to arrive at no and remain there.

To say no can often be an ordeal. It becomes even more difficult
when the body is accustomed to accepting the no-good man's
excuses for avoiding responsibility. However, where there is a will,
there is a way. And if a woman has finally come to acknowledge that
she is, indeed, involved with a no-good man, then this section will
prepare her mind and body to take a stand.

There must be certain revelations before embarking upon this
journey. First, a woman needs to realize that success begins with
self. Belief in the body's ability to achieve will allow for the hidden
potential and strength to take control. The second thing that must
occur is the removal of *can't* from the vocabulary. For when the
mind thinks it cannot, then the body will not.

The mind leads and the body follows. Liberate the mind and the
body will follow. That phrase captures the essence of mental
strength, which involves structuring the mind to be firm, uncom-
promising, and disciplined. This decreases the vulnerability of the
mind to be influenced by outside factors. It begins with the mind of
an individual knowing where its capabilities lie, accompanied by the
belief that there is the ability to apply them to the situation at hand.
But in order to access this strength, it is imperative that a woman
take love out of the decision-making process. Thus the heart must
be restricted from involvement in determining what needs to be
done.

In order to confront this struggle, a woman must be willing to
place one hundred percent of her effort into this. As in the qualities
or ingredients needed to form a realationship, her intent and inter-

nal focus must be genuine and real. Not only must the woman be honest with herself, but she must also devote herself to saying no and to her healing process, never allowing anything to make her stray away from the task at hand.

Saying no should not be something that a woman does for the sake of those around her, because she feels the need to prove her strength to everyone but herself. The woman must want to say no because she is sick and tired of being abused. She is sick and tired of being neglected. The woman must want to say no because she feels that enough is enough and she has reached her boiling point. She must want to say no because she knows that she is worth it and not worthless. And last but most importantly, the woman must want to say no because the love she has for herself outweighs the love that she has for someone who shows no love toward her.

A woman must realize that thinking no and saying no are two different things. Once the mind thinks no and transfers that thought to the body, allowing the woman to open up her mouth and tell that no-good man no, either for the first or last time and actually mean business, she has to be strong and firm in her speech. There must be no action or body language that implies yes, whether it is by way of a smile, a hug, or terms of endearment. The woman must look the no-good man straight in his eyes. She must not blink or sweat. She should say it's over with calm and confidence, then leave. The woman should not explain why she has come to this conclusion. She should not allow for him to respond with false promises. After all is said and done, she must walk away and stay away.

Once a woman arrives at no, then her body must stick to it. Become accustomed to saying no. Saying no and then not leaving, allows him to call the woman's bluff. If success is what a woman seeks, she should prepare herself for the comebacks, follow-up phone calls, visits, or reasons that he will offer as an explanation to take him back. Because the woman has probably been dealing with his nonsense for some time already, she will have a good idea of what to expect and should properly prepare herself. I encourage the woman to give him back all of his things. Get rid of everything that has any memories linked to him. This will free the body and allow for it to remain in freedom.

Once a woman learns how to say no in the English language, learning 999 additional ways to tell the no-good man no will be a breeze. Nonetheless, I must warn some women to proceed with caution. If the no-good man in question happens to be the "laying of the hands" type, in order to save yourself an ambulance ride, you might want to skip the direct confrontation and just leave.

14

999 Ways
2
Say No
2
a
No-Good Man

Sega, Zadna, Nee, and Sinalubiri are all forms of expression that may create feelings of eeriness. But on the contrary, the need to say them is rooted in something very serious.

Yes, the English language is direct and precise. But variety is known to be the spice of life. Therefore, 999 additional ways to tell the no-good man no is an extremely gratifying thing. And although intelligence may be something that the mind of the no-good man rejects, like the body rejects an organ after surgery, the woman should still never fear to expose his mind to some linguistically stimulating information. Thus, when he barks to ask, "What does that mean?" tell him to do something useful with his time and look it up.

*Note: There are more than 6,000 known languages, but only about 2,000 have a written system. The following represents those that are the most commonly spoken. These languages are spoken in a variety of regions. Nonetheless, the languages listed are not necessarily limited to the specified areas.

Languages of Africa and the Middle East

Afar <Ethiopia>: Maley
Afrikaans <South Africa>: Nee
Afrikaans: Geen
Akkadian <Eastern and Northern Africa>: La
Amharic <Ethiopia, Israel, and Egypt >: Aye
Amharic: Aydelem
Amharic: Yelem
Amharic: Ie
Arabic <Middle East and North Africa>: La
Arabic: Lela
Arabic: Lay
Arabic: Laa
Armenian <Armenia>: Che
Armenian: Voch
Asante <Ghana>: Daabi
Ashkun <Afghanistan>: Ma
Assyrian <Iraq, Syria, and Iran>: La
Ateso <Uganda>: Mam

Bagesu <Central African Congo>: Ah ah
Bagesu: Sinalubiri
Bagirmi <Chad and Nigeria>: Eli
Baka Pygmy <Cameroon and Gabon>: De
Baka: Ode
Bakitara <Central Africa>: Nangwa
Balochi <Pakistan>: Enna
Bambara <Mali, Gambia, and Senegal>: Ayi
Basabei <Central Africa>: Katai
Basabei: Kutai
Bemba <Zambia>: Awe
Bengali <Bangladesh>: Na

Bete <Cameroon>: Bobo
Bobangi <Congo>: Te
Boboda <Mali and Burkina Faso>: Ao
Brahui <Afghanistan>: All
Bukusu <Kenya>: Taawe
Bulu <Cameroon>: Momo
Burushashki <Pakistan>: Bee ya
Burushashki: Be
Burushashki: Bee

Chichewa <South Africa and Malawi>: Iyaye
Chichewa: Iyayi
Chinyanja <Malawi>: Iyayi
Chinyanja: Íài
Chitonga <Zambia>: Pepe
Comori <Comoros>: La
Congo <Zaire>: Vê

Dagaare <Ghana>: Ai
Dinka <Sudan>: Aliu
Diola <Senegal>: Hani

Egyptian <Egypt>: Ma
Ekegusii <Kenya>: Aa
Emakhua <Mozambique>: Kha
Eton <Cameroon>: Me to benn
Ewondo <Cameroon>: Koa

Fang <Gabon>: Koko
Fangalo <South Africa>: Cha
Fante <Ghana>: Aaha
Fon <Benin>: Eo

Fulani <Burkina Faso and Niger Republic>: Ala
Fulfude <Nigeria>: Ta
Fur <Chad and Sudan>: Aba

Gaam <Sudan>: Wà
Ganda <Uganda>: Nedda
Ganda: Aaà
Gujarati <Kenya, Pakistan, Uganda, and Tanzania> Nahiin

Harari <Ethiopia>: Me
Hausa <Nigeria>: Babu
Hebrew <Israel>: Lo

Icetot <Uganda>: Ntondo
IsiNdebele <South Africa>: Awa
IsiXhosa <South Africa>: Hayi
IsiZulu <South Africa>: Cha

Kabuverdianu <West Africa and Cape Verde>: Nau
Kabyle <Algeria>: Ak
Kamviri <Afghanistan>: N'a'i
Kanuri <Nigeria, Sudan, Cameroon, and Chad>: Aa
Kashmiri <Pakistan>: Ma
Kashmiri: Ne-keh
Kiga <Niger-Congo>: Ingaaha
Kikongo <Angola and Republic of Congo>: Vê
Kikuyu <Kenya>: Aca
Kikuyu: Tiguo
Kiluba <Zaire>: Aa
Kinyarwanda <Rwanda>: Oya
Kipsigis <Kenya>: Acha
Kirundi <Burundi>: Oya

Kisanga <Zaire>: Yo
Kiswahili <South Africa>: Hapana
Kiswahili: A-a
Khakea <Botswana and Namibia>: Taku
Khowar <Pakistan>: No
Khowar: Moh
Kohistani <Pakistan and Afghanistan>: Ni
Koromfe <Burkina Faso>: Ajo
Koromfe: Ajej
Kunama <Eritrea and Ethiopia>: Dima
Kunama: Immi imme
Kung-ekoka <Angola>: Kúa
Kung-ekoka: Kúi
Kurdi <Iran and Iraq>: Na
Kurdi: Ne
Kurdi: Neu
Kwanyama <Angola and Namibia>: Aaye
Kwanyama: Ahawe
Kwanyama: Ahowe
Kweyol <Botswana and Namibia>: Kwa

Ladakhi <Pakistan>: Man
Ladakhi: Biduk
Lingala <Angola>: Té
Lugbara <Democratic Republic of Congo and Uganda>: Ko
Lunda <Zambia>: Inehi
Lunyankole <Uganda>: Ngaaha
Lunyoro <Uganda>: Kwaha
Luo <Sudan and Kenya>: Ooyo
Luvale <Zambia>: Kagute

Malagasy <Madagascar>: An an
Malagasy: Tsia
Mampruli <Ghana>: Ai
Mandinka <Gambia and Senegal>: Hani
Masai <Kenya and Tanzania>: Mme
Mashi <Botswana>: Nanga
Mende <Sierra Leone>: A-a
Mina <Togo>: Ao
Mofu-Gudur <Cameroon>: Ba
Moore <Burkina Faso>: Ayo

Nama <Botswana, Namibia, and South Africa>: Tama
Nandi <Kenya>: Achicha
Ndebele <South Africa>: Hayi
Ngbaka <Northern Congo and Zaire>: Ùú
Nigerian <Nigeria>: No
Nupe <Nigeria>: Áà
Nupe: Àwâ

Otetela <Congo>: Mbu

Pashto <Pakistan and Afghanistan>: Na
Pashto: Nakhayr
Pende <Congo and Zaire>: M'khu
Persian <Iran and Afghanistan>: Nah
Punjabi Western <United Arab Emirates, Afghanistan, and Pakistan>: Na
Pulaar <Guinea, Ethiopia, Senegal, Gambia, and Mali>: Wonaa

Sango <Central African Republic>: Ipo
Sarangambay <Chad>: Waa
Sepedi <South Africa>: Aowa

Sesotho <South Africa>: Tjhee
Sesotho: Aikona
Sesotho: Tjhe
Setswana <South Africa>: Nyaa
Shimasiwa <Comoros>: Uh uh
Shona <Zimbabwe>: Aiwa
Shona: Kwete
Shuwa <Chad, Cameroon, Niger, and Nigeria>: Ma
Silozi <Zambia>: Baatili
Sindhi <Pakistan>: Ma
Sindhi: Na
Siswati <Swaziland>: Ha
Somali <Somalia>: Maya
Soninke <Mali and Senegal>: Ayi
Sudanese <Sudan>: Heunteu
Sudanese: Ulah
Sudanese: Sanes
Swahili <Eastern Africa>: Katu
Swahili: Hasha
Swazi <Swaziland>: Ha

Tagargrent <Algeria>: Ou
Tamashek <Mali>: Kala-kala
Tarifit <Algeria and Morocco>: La
Tarifit: Ur
Tedaga <Libya, Chad, Niger, and Nigeria>: Si
Tedaga: Sa
Tigre <Ethiopia>: La'
Tigre: Lala'
Tosk <Egypt and Albania>: Nuk
Tschiluba <Zaire>: To
Tshivenda <South Africa>: Hai

Tsonga <South Africa>: E-e
Twi <Ghana>: Daabí

Uzbek <Afghanistan>: Yuk
Uzbek: Yöq

Wakhi <Afghanistan>: Neis
Wali <Ghana>: Aye
Wolof <Senegal, Mali, Gambia, and Guinea>: Deedeet

Yeyi <Namibia and Botswana>: Iyemwaa
Yoruba < Nigeria and Benin>: Oti
Yoruba: Rara
Yoruba: Béè kó

Zande <Sudan, Central African Republic, and Congo>: Te
Zande: Ya
Zarmaci <Mali, Niger and Benin>: Si
Zulu <South Africa>: Haai ngeko

Languages Of Asia

Abun <Indonesia>: Nde
Akha <Thailand, Laos, Burma, Thailand, and Vietnam>: Mah nguh
Aklanon <Philippines>: Indi
Amis <Taiwan>: Cuwa
Apabhramsha <India>: Ma
Apuchikwar <India>: Poyeda
Atayal <Taiwan>: Iyat

Basque <Philippines>: Ez
Batak <Philippines, Indonesia, and Sumatra>: Daong
Bauzi <Indonesia>: Kai
Bojigiab <India>: Poi-e
Bru <Thailand>: Taah
Bugi <Indonesia and Malaysia>: Mu
Burmese <Myanmar>: Mahou' pabu
Burmese: Mahou' hpu

Cantonese <China>: Mhai
Cebuano <Philippines>: Dili
Cham <Cambodia and Vietnam>: Ô

Dawan <Indonesia>: Kaha'
Dhivehi <Maldives>: Noon
Dusun <Malaysia>: A' ou

Ekari <Indonesia>: Beu
Evenki <China>: Aachin

Gujarati <India>: Ma
Gujarati: Naa

Gujarati: Nahiin
Gurung <Nepal, India, and Bhutan >: Ah nglhq

Hakka <China> Mo
Hiligaynon <Philippines>: Indi
Hindi <India>: Ji nahi
Hindi: Nahin
Hindi: Ji nahin
Hindi: Naheen
Hindi: Hye
Hindustani <India>: Na
Hmong <Vietnam>: Chui mua
Hmong <Thailand and Laos>: Tsis
Hoi San <China>: M hai
Hokkien <Taiwan>: Bo
Hokkien: M si an-ne
Hokkien <Indonesia and Singapore>: Msi

Ibatan <Philippines>: Ava
Ilokano <Philippines>: Haan
Ilokano: Saan
Indonesian <Indonesia>: Tidak
Indonesian: Ndak
Indonesian: Kagak
Indonesian: Nggak
Indonesian: Jangan
Itbayaten <Philippines>: Engga
Ivasayen <Phillippines>: Omba

Japanese <Japan>: Iie
Javanese <Indonesia, Singapore, and Malaysia>: Mboten

Javanese: Ora
Javenese: Sanes

Kadazan <Malaysia>: A'ou
Kalasha <India>: Ne
Kalasha: Moh
Kannada <India>: Beda
Kannada: Illa
Kapampangan <Philippines>: Ali
Karen <Burma>: Mwe é
Kazakh <China>: Zhoq
Kharia <Nepal and India>: Abu
Khmer <Cambodia>: Te
Khmer: Ot te
Khmu <Laos>: Pa
Konkani <India>: Naa
Korean <Korea>: Aniyo
Korean: Animnida
Kumamoto <Japan>: Nne
Kurukh <India>: Mala
Kyo Kotoba <Japan>: Iya

Lahu <Thailand>: Mah hey
Lao <Laos>: Bo
Lepcha <Nepal, India, and Bhutan>: Megun

Malay <Malaysia>: Bukan
Malay: Aucun
Malay: Tidak
Malayalam <Indonesia, India, and Singapore>: Al
Manchu <China>: Waka
Manchu: Aku

Mandarin <China>: Bu shi zhe yang
Mandarin: Bu dui
Mandarin: Bu shi
Mandarin: Meiyou
Mang < Thailand, Vietnam, and China>: Ham
Marathi <India>: Nahi
Marin <Indonesia>: Baken
Mien <Vietnam>: M'i mái
Mien <Thailand and Laos>: Maiv
Mien: Mv
Minangkabau <Indonesia>: Indak
Mlabri <Thailand and Laos>: Met
Mon <Burma>: Hùe
Mon <Thailand>: Ha
Mongolian <Mongolia>: Ügüi
Mongolian: Bish
Mundari <Nepal and India>: Ka

Naxi <China>: Me waq
Nepali <Nepal>: Ahaa
Nepali: Hoina
Nepali: Chaina
Newari <Nepal>: Makhu

Orya <Indonesia>: Bahem
Ossetian <Central Asia and Caucasus>: Noun
Ossetian: Nö
Ossetian: Næ

Pampangan <Philippines>: Ali
Pangan <Malaysia>: Ning
Pangan: Neng

Pangasinan <Philippines>: Ag
Pangasinan: Aliwan
Pangasinan: Andi
Punjabi <India>: Naheen
Punjabi: Nahi

Sadan Toraja <Indonesia>: Tae
Sakai <Malaysia>: Täto to
Sakai: Tahatna
Santali <Nepal, India, and Bhutan>: Banj
Sasak <Indonesia>: Nde
Sema <India>: Mo
Semelai <Malaysia>: Beh
Sendaiben <Japan>: Yanda
Sherpa <Tibet and Nepal>: Ahha
Sherpa: Mecheye
Sherpa: Me sheki
Shina <India>: Neh
Sinhalese <Sri Lanka>: Natha

Tabla <Indonesia>: Pai
Tagalog <Philippines>: Hindi po
Tagalog: Hindi
Tamil <India>: Illai
Tamil: Venda
Tatar <China>: Yuk
Tay <Vietnam>: Boomi
Telugu <India>: Kaddu
Telugu: Ledu
Thai <Thailand>: Maidai
Thai: Maichai
Thai: Mai

Thai: Maioua
Tibetan <Tibet and China>: Marey
Tibetan: Yo
Tibetan: Meyin
Tosaben <Japan>: Ingeno
Tukang Besi <Indonesia>: Mbe'ae
Tulu <India>: Ijji
Tulu: Iddi

Una <Indonesia>: Kum
Una: Xum
Urdu <India and Pakistan>: Nahin
Urdu: Nehiin
Uyghur <China>: Jyok
Uyghur: Yaq

Vietnamese <Vietnam>: Không
Vietnamese: Thua không
Visayan <Philippines>: Dili
Visayan: Tifale

Waigali <India>: Mi

Yamagata <Japan>: Nne
Yao <China, Thailand, and Laos>: Ngava
Yugur <China>: Yahq

Zhuang <China>: Bow
Zhurzhen <China>: Ejxe

Languages of Australia and Islands of the Pacific

Abasakur <Papua New Guinea>: Oya
Alamblak <Papua New Guinea>: Na ne
Alyawarr <Australia>: Arangkwa
Ama <Papua New Guinea>: Wei mu
Ambulas <Papua New Guinea>: Kapwk
Amele <Papua New Guinea>: P
Ami <Australia>: Way
Ampeeli-Wojokeso <Papua New Guinea>: Maaha
Amto <Papua New Guinea>: Hemyek
Angaathia <Papua New Guinea>: Maae
Anindilyakwa <Australia>: Nari
Ankave <Papua New Guinea>: Fima
Awa <Papua New Guinea>: Akq áho
Awa: Aqa

Bagandji <Australia>: Gila
Bahinemo <Papua New Guinea>: Mbaya
Bamu <Papua New Guinea>: Puaie
Bandjalang <Australia>: Yagam
Bandjalang: Yugam
Barai <Papua New Guinea>: Naembe
Barai: Kumbe
Bargam <Papua New Guinea>: Haigam
Baruya <Papua New Guinea>: Ma ymiko
Beami <Papua New Guinea>: Name
Benabena <Papua New Guinea>: Me
Bidyara <Australia>: Gara
Bine <Papua New Guinea>: Lika
Boikin <Papua New Guinea>: Mapm
Bugotu <Solomon Islands>: Teo
Bukiyip <Papua New Guinea>: Wa

Bukyip: Moda
Bunaba <Australia>: Ngai
Burum Mindik <Papua New Guinea>: Kpahp

Chamorro <Guam>: Ahe'

Dadibi <Papua New Guinea>: Mni
Daga <Papua New Guinea>: Ae
Daga: Ya
Daga: Uon
Dano: <Papua New Guinea>: Ove
Dhangu <Australia>: Yagu
Diyari <Australia>: Wata
Djamindjung <Australia>: Guran
Djapu <Australia>: Yaga
Duna <Papua New Guinea>: Neya
Dyirbal <Australia>: Yimba

Enga <Papua New Guinea>: Daá
English <Australia>: Nut

Falopo <Papua New Guinea>: Maibo
Fasu <Papua New Guinea>: Wai
Fijian <Fiji Islands>: Sega
Fore <Papua New Guinea>: Aa
Fore: Kampa

Gamilaraay <Australia>: Gamil
Gimi <Papua New Guinea>: Kakare
Giramay <Australia>: Maya
Guhu Samane <Papua New Guinea>: Bamu
Gumatj <Australia>: Yaka

Gumbaynggir <Australia>: Biway
Gundungurra <Australia>: Gurrangung
Guniyandi <Australia>: Manari

Houailou <Fiji Islands>: Aè

Iatmul <Papua New Guinea>: Kay
Imonda <Papua New Guinea>: Auaia
Imonda: Xoi

Kala Kawaw Ya <Australia>: Lawnga
Kalamai <Australia>: Kuru
Kaliai Kove <Papua New Guinea>: Mao
Kaliai Kove: Mako
Kamano <Papua New Guinea>: Ao
Kamasau <Papua New Guinea>: Segyi
Kapingamarangi <Pacific Islands>: Deeai
Karkar Yuri <Papua New Guinea>: Mn
Kate <Papua New Guinea>: Aricne
Kaurareg <Australia>: Lawnga
Kewa East <Papua New Guinea>: Dia
Kewa West <Papua New Guinea>: Na
Kissi <Papua New Guinea>: Re
Kobon <Papua New Guinea>: Wase
Koiari <Papua New Guinea>: Bebe
Koiali <Papua New Guinea>: Xoli
Komba <Papua New Guinea>: Ma
Korafe <Papua New Guinea>: Era
Kosraean <Micronesia>: Moh
Kriol <Australia>: Nomo
Kukatja <Australia>: Wiya
Kutthung <Australia>: Gooran

Kwoma <Papua New Guinea>: Yaho
Kwoma: Saka

Lenakel <Pacific Islands>: Kapwa
Leningitij <Australia>: Ngga'

Mabuiag <Australia>: Lawnga
Macedonian <Macedonia>: Ne
Mae <Pacific Islands>: Ikai
Magindano <Papua New Guinea>: Dele
Maia <Papua New Guinea>: Wyek
Manambu <Papua New Guinea>: Ma
Maohi <South Pacific Islands>: Aita
Maori <New Zealand>: Kao
Maori <Cook Islands>: Kare
Maridjabin <Australia>: Ampi
Marimanindji <Australia>: Mampi
Maringgar <Australia>: Ampu
Marshallese <Marshall Islands>: Jaab
Meriam Mir <Australia>: Nole
Mullukmulluk <Australia>: Akana

Nabak <Papua New Guinea>: Ku
Nangikurrunggurr <Australia>: Minta
Nauruan <Oceania>: Iòk
Nauruan: Deò ei
Ndjebbana <Australia>: Koma
Ngadjonji <Australia>: Ngarru
Ngadjunma <Australia>: Jowandjan
Nhirrpi <Australia>: Warrayi
Nobanob <Papua New Guinea>: Ida

Nukuoro <Pacific Islands>: Deai
Nyungar <Australia>: Juat

Oksapmin <Papua New Guinea>: Na
Ono <Papua New Guinea>: Mi
Orokaiva <Papua New Guinea>: Mane
Orokola <Papua New Guinea>: Ka
Orokola: Lue
Owiniga <Papua New Guinea>: Naburu

Paamese <Vanuatu>: Vuo
Paamese: Vuol
Paamese: Vuel
Pakanh <Australia>: Ya'a
Pappua <Papua New Guinea>: Roba
Pijin <Solomon Islands>: No
Pijin: Nomoa
Pitjantjatjara <Australia>: Wiya
Polynesian <Islands of Polynesia>: Si'ai
Polynesian: Siei
Pulawat <Micronesia>: Yaapw
Pulawat: Mmm
Pulawat: Yeehee
Puoc <Australia>: Pa
Purari <Papua New Guinea>: Aii
Purari: Peo

Rao <Papua New Guinea>: Was
Rarotongan <South Pacific Islands>: Kare
Rotokas <Papua New Guinea>: Biapau
Rotuman <Fiji Islands>: Igka'I

Rotuman: Igke'i
Roviana <Solomon Islands>: Lokari

Samo <Papua New Guinea>: Mi
Samoan <Samoa Islands>: Leai
Selepet <Papua New Guinea>: Ki
Siroi <Papua New Guinea>: Kwa

Tahitan <Tahiti>: Aita
Tairora <Papua New Guinea>: Aau
Tairora: Kia
Tarawan <Oceania>: Akêa
Timbo <Papua New Guinea>: Bo
Tjalkadjara <Australia>: Tailpa
Toaripi <Papua New Guinea>: Kau
Tok Pisin <Papua New Guinea>: Nogat
Tongan <Pacific Islands>: Ikai
Trobes Tokples <Papua New Guinea>: Gala

Usan <Papua New Guinea>: Ue

Wagiman <Australia>: Wihya
Waljen <Australia>: Wandi
Wangaaybuwan Ngiyambaa <Australia>: Wangaay
Wangaaybuwan Ngiyambaa: Wayil
Waskia <Papua New Guinea>: Mna
Wik Mungkan <Australia>: Ya'a
Wiradjuri <Australia>: Wirraay

Yagaria <Papua New Guinea>: Ee
Yareba <Papua New Guinea>: Me
Yele <Papua New Guinea>: Kel

Yindjibarndi <Australia>: Mita
Yolngu Matha <Australia>: Yaka
Yumpla Tok <Australia>: No

Languages of Europe

Adyghe <Russia>: Hawaa
Adyghe: Haw
Akkadian <Assyria>: Ul
Albanian <Albania>: Jo
Alsacian <France>: Ne
Altai <Russia>: Jok
Arberesh <Italy>: Jo
Aromunian <Greece>: Nu
Asturian <Spain>: Non
Asturian: Nun
Avar <Russia, Azerbaijan, and Turkey>: Heo
Azeri <Turkey, Turkmen>: Yox

Bashkir <Russia and Ukraine>: Yok
Basque <France and Spain>: Ez
Belarusian: <Belarus, Poland, and Latvia>: Ne
Belarusian: Nie
Bosnian <Bosnia>: Ne
Bosnian: Hm
Breton <France>: Nann
Breton: Ket
Brigidian <Ireland>: Nope
Bulgarian <Bulgaria>: Ne

Cassubian <Poland>: Nie'
Catalan <Andorra, France, and Spain>: No
Chuvash <Russia>: Chuk
Cornish <England>: Nag eus
Cornish: Na
Cornish: Nag usy

Croatian <Bosnia and Croatia>: Ne
Czech <Czech Republic>: Zadna

Danish <Denmark and Greenland>: Ingenlunde
Danish: Nej
Dutch <Netherlands and Belguim>: Nee
Dutch: Neen
Dutch: Geen
Dutch: Niet

Erzya <Russia>: A
Esperanto <France>: Ne
Estonian <Estonia>: Ei
Estonian: Ep
Estonian: Es
Estonian: Eiba
Estonian: Eih
Estonian: Õih
Etruscan <Roman Italian>: Ein
Even <Russia>: Aan
Even: Aach

Faroese <Denmark>: Ikki
Faroese: Nei
Farsi <Tajikistan>: Ne
Finnish <Finland, Estonia, and Norway>: Ei
Flemish <Belgium, France, and Netherlands>: Nee
French <France>: Non
French: Pas
French: Surtout pas
French: Ne nulle
Frisian <Germany>: Nee

Friulian <Italy>: Nò
Furlan <Eastern Europe>: No

Gagauz <Moldova, Romania, Ukraine, and Bulgaria>: Diyl yola
Galician <Spain>: Non
Gallo <France>: Nenni
Gallo: Nona
Gallo: Nani
Gascon <France>: Nani
Georgian <Georgia>: Ah-ra
Georgian: Ara
German <Germany>: Nein
German: Kein
German: Keineswegs
German <Austria>: Naa
German: Nö
German <Germany>: Nee
German <Switzerland>: Nei
German: Naa
German <Bavaria>: Na
Greek <Greece>: Ochi
Griko <Italy>: Nã' ã

Hungarian <Hungary>: Visszautasitas
Hungarian: Nem

Icelandic <Iceland>: Nei
Indo European: Ne
Ingush <Russia>: Aa
Inuttut <Greenland>: Naamik
Irish <Ireland>: Nil
Irish: Ní hea

Ishkashmi <Tajikistan>: No
Ishkashmi: Ne
Italian <Italy>: No

Kalmyk <Russia>: Uga
Karachay Balkar <Armenia, Kazakhstan, and Russia>: Tuyul
Karelian <Finland and Russia>: Ei
Khakas <Russia>: Chox
Kirgiz <Kyrgyzstan>: Jok
Komi Permyak <Russia>: Aga
Komi Zyryan <Russia>: Abu

Lak <Ukraine and Georgia>: Qa
Latin <Ancient Rome>: Non
Latin: Nullus
Latin: Minime
Latvian <Latvia, Sweden, Lithuania, Belarus, and Ukraine>: Ne
Lingua Franca <Mediterranean>: No
Lingua Franca: Non
Lithuanian <Lithuania>: Ne
Lithuanian: A'a
Lithuanian: M'm
Livonian <Livonia and Estonia>: Äb
Livonian: Ät
Low Saxon <Germany>: Nee
Luxembourgeois <Luxemburg, Belgium, France, and Germany>: Net
Luxemburgish <Luxemburg>: Neen
Luxemburgish: Nee

Maltese <Malta, United Kingdom, and Italy>: Le
Mansi <Russia>: Aat

Mari <Russia>: Uke
Monegasque <Monaco>: Non
Mordvin <Russia>: Aras
Mordvin: Ajaš
Mordvin: Aš
Mundes <Germany>: Menga

Nanai <Russia>: Edi
Nanai: Ana
Nenets <Russia>: Ya'ngo
Norwegian <Norway>: Ikke
Norwegian: Næi
Norwegian: Nei

Occitan <France, Spain, and Italy>: No
Orok <Russia>: Ana

Plattdeutsch <Germany>: Nau
Plattdeutsch: Nee
Polish <Poland>: Nie
Portuguese <Portugal>: Não
Provencal <France>: Non
Provencal: Nani
Prussian <Prussia>: Ni

Romani <Bulgaria>: Na
Romanian <Romania>: Nu
Romansch <Switzerland>: Na
Romany <Eastern and Western Europe>: Kek
Russian <Russia>: Nyet

Saami <Scandinavia and Russia>: Ále
Saami Davvi <Scandinavia>: Ii
Saami: Ij
Sardinian <Italy>: No
Sarnami <Holland and Suriname>: Na
Savonian <Finland>: Ee
Scots <Scotland>: Naw
Scots: Nae
Scots <Ireland>: Na
Serbian <Yugoslavia and Bosnia>: Ne
Setu <Estonia>: Õiõ
Sicilian <Italy>: Nuddu
Sicilian: Nessunu
Slovak <Slovakia>: Nie
Slovenian <Slovenia>: Ne
Sorbian <Germany>: Ne
Spanish <Spain>: No
Sursilvan <Switzerland>: Na
Swabian <Germany>: Noe
Swedish <Sweden and Finland>: Nej

Tajik <Tajikistan>: Ne
Tashkorghani <Turkey>: Nay
Tatar <Russia>: Yuk
Turkish <Turkey>: Hayir
Turkmen <Turkmenistan>: Yok
Tuvan <Russia>: Chok

Udmurt <Russia>: Övöl
Ukranian <Ukraine>: Ni
Ulcha <Russia>: Ana

Valencian <Spain>: No
Veps <Russia>: Ei
Voltic <Russia>: Ei
Voltic: EB
Voltic: Ep

Wallon <Belgium>: Nenni
Welsh <Wales>: Na

Yiddish <Hungary, Israel, and Russia>: Neyn
Yiddish: Nit

Languages of North America

Abenaki <Native American-Western Maine and Canada>: Nda
Abenaki: Ôda
Agua Caliente <Native American-California>: Gai
Alabamu <Native American-Texas>: Ánkobi
American English: Get Away Before I Take Out My Pepper Spray!
American English: Leave My Face Before I Take Out My Mace!
American English: Nick Nat Patty Wack Give A Dog A NO!
American English: (Sometimes To Reach A Dog, You Have To Speak His Language) Roof!
American English: Roof, Roof!
Amuzgo <Mexico>: Ti
Apache <Native American-Arizona>: Dah
Ayticha Yokuts <Native American-California>: Gatu

Biloxi <Mississippi Valley>: Ni
Blackfoot <Native American-Montana and Canada>: Saa

Cahita <Mexico>: E
Cahita: Ee
Cahita: É' e
Cahto <Native American-California>: Doo-yee
Cahuilla <Native American-Southern California>: Kily
Cahuilla: Kí'i
Cahuilla: E
Chemehuevi <Native American-California>: Ka'c
Chemehuevi: Ka'cu
Cherokee <Native American-North Carolina and Oklahoma>: Tla
Cherokee: Tla-hv
Cherokee: V'-tla
Cheyenne <Native American-Montana>: Hová'åháne
Chinook <Native American-Columbia River>: Halo

Chinook: Wake
Chinook: No
Choctaw <Native American-Oklahoma>: Keyu
Choctaw: Ahanh
Choctaw: Chikimba
Choctaw: Iksho
Chol <Mexico>: Mach
Chol: Ma'anic
Chol: Ma'
Chowchilla <Native American-California>: Ohom
Choynimni Yokuts <Native American-California>: K'amu
Choynok <Native American-California>: Ohom
Chumash <Native American-California>: Anictu
Chumash: Sewilx
Chumash: Pwo
Chumash: Se
Chumash: Amo
Cochimi <Mexico>: Nyi
Comanche <Native American-Southwest Oklahoma>: Kai
Comanche: Keka
Comanche: Tocusé
Costanoan <Native American-Central California>: Kue
Costanoan: Akwi
Costanoan: Ekwe
Costanoan: Elekic
Cree <Canada>: Mwâc
Cree: Namôya
Cree: Mola
Creek <Native American-Oklahoma and Florida>: Kus
Creek: Mónkos
Creek: Hekúst
Creole <Haiti>: Non

Crow <Native American-Missouri River>: Sa
Crow: Su
Crow: Déta

Dekelh <Canada>: Andooh
Dekelh: Awundooh
Diegueno <Native American-Southern California>: Umaaw

Emdimbich <Native American-California>: Gadu
Esselen < Native American-Central California>: Me' tea
Esselen: A'na
Eudeve <Mexico>: Quéta

Fernandino <Native American-California>: Xai

Gabrielino <Native American-California>: Xai
Gashowu Yokuts <Native American-California>: K'amu
Gitanemuk <Native American-California>: Nau

Haida <Alaska>: Aya
Hawaiian <Hawaii>: A'ole
Hidatsa <Native American-North Dakota>: Desa
Hidatsa: Nesats
Hnahnu <Mexico>: Hina
Hometwoli Yokuts <Native American-California>: Uhun
Hopi <Native American-Northeast Arizona>: Qa'é
Hopi: Gae'
Hopi: K'ae'
Huastec <Mexico>: Ib
Huave <Mexico>: Ngwüy
Huave: Ngome
Huichol <Mexico>: Ka

Innu <Canada>: Maawaach
Inuktitut <Native American-Canada and Alaska>: Aakka
Inuktitut: Naaga
Inuktitut: Aagaa
Inuktitut: Naaka
Itza <Mexico>: Ma'
Ixcatec <Mexico>: Na
Ixcatex: A

Juaneno <Native American-Southern California>: Kayon

Kathlamet <Native American-Oregon>: Ka'ya
Kawaiisu <California>: Kètô
Kechayi Yokuts <Native American-California>: Ohom
Kosati <Native American-Oklahoma and Alabama>: Iniko
Kreyol <Haiti>: Okenn
Kurak <Native American-California>: Puuhara

Laiman <Native American>: Ñi
Lakhota <Canada>: Hiya
Lakhota: Shnee
La Perouse <Native American-California>: Maal
Lenape <Native American-Delaware>: Mata
Luiseno <Native American-Southern California>: Qay
Luiseno: Gai
Lushootseed <Native American-Washington>: Xwí

Michahay Yokuts <Native American-California>: Gâmu
Michif <Canada>: Noo
Michif: Pa miyeur
Mikmaq <Canada>: Moqwa

Mingo <Native American-Ohio and West Virginia>: Hee
Miwok <Native American-Central California>: Ewutû
Miwok: Hama
Miwok: Hella
Mixe <Mexico>: Ka'p
Mixe: Ka
Mixe: Kiáp
Mixtec <Mexico>: Koó
Mixtec: Tú'
Mixtec: Túu
Mobilian <Native American-Gulf of Mexico, Florida, and Texas>
Ekshu
Modoc <Native American-California>: Q'ay
Mohineyam <Native American-California>: Nau
Mono <Native American-East and Central California>: Karu
Mono: Gadu
Mono: Garu

Nahuatl <Mexico>: Amo
Nakota <Canada>: Hiya
Navajo <Native American-Arizona>: Dooda
Navajo: Ndaga'
Nutunutu Yokuts <Native American-California>: Ohò'm

Ofo <Native American-Lower Mississippi Valley>: Ni
Ojibwe <North Canada>: Gaawesa
Osage <Native American-Northern Plains >: Hon' ka zhi
Osage: On' ka zhi

Pame <Mexico>: Mwi
Papiamentu <Aruba, British Virgin Islands, and Puerto Rico>: No
Passamaqoddy <Native American-Maine>: Kotama

Passamaqoddy: Konotiri
Passamaqoddy: Ne
Paviotso <Native American-California>: Karu
Phorhepecha <Mexico>: Ámbe
Phorhepecha: Ási
Phorhepecha: Ástarhu
Pima <Mexico>: Pia'a
Pomo <Native American-Central California>: Kui
Popoloca <Mexico>: Da'
Popoloca: Caj
Potawatomi <Native American-Northern and Central USA>: Co

Saanich <Canada>: Ewe
San Juan Capistrano <Native American-California>: Kai
Seri <Mexico>: Saate
Serrano <Native American-Southern California>: Nou
Shikaviyam <Native American-California>: Gè
Shoshoni <Native American-Montana, Idaho, Utah, Arizona, and Nevada>: Kai
Spanish <Puerto Rico and Dominican Republic>: No
Spokane <Native American-Washington State>: Tá

Taino <Caribbean and Florida>: U'a
Taino: Wu'a
Tarahumara <Mexico>: Ké
Tarahumara: Que
Tarahumara: Tarapé
Tepehua <Mexico>: Maitague
Tlahuica <Mexico>: T'akwha
Tlingit <Alaska>: Tleix
Tojolabal <Mexico>: Miyuc
Tojolabal: Mi

Tongva <Native American-California>: Hí ekh
Totonac <Mexico>: Nichuna
Tseshaht <Canada>: Wik
Tubatulabal <Native American-California>: Haic
Tulamni Yokuts <Native American-California>: Anhan
Tzeltal <Mexico>: Ju'uk
Tzeltal: Mo'oj
Tzutujil <Mexico>: Maan
Tzutujil: Ma

Ute <Native American-Utah and Colorado>: Kach

Washo <Native American-California>: Ès
Wechihit Yokuts <Native American-California>: Ohòm
Winnemem Wintu <Native American-California>: El eh oh
Wintu <Native American-California>: Min
Wintu: Mina
Wiyot <Native American-California>: Kia
Wukchamni Yokuts <Native American-California>: K'amu

Yaqui <Mexico>: È'e
Yawdanchi Yokuts <Native American-California>: K'amu
Yawelmani Yokuts <Native American-California>: Ohom
Yucatec Maya <Mexico>: Ma'
Yucatec Maya: Maa
Yuki <Native American-California>: Tan
Yuki: Mi tang keh
Yupik <Native American-Alaska>: Ganga

Zapotec <Mexico>: Que
Zapotec: Akti
Zapotec: Cabi

Zoque <Mexico>: Watkáh
Zoque: Ja'ne
Zuni <Native American-Southwest USA>: Ella

Languages of South America and Central America

Acateco <Guatemala>: K'amaj
Achi <Guatemala>: Ntaj
Achuar <Ecuador>: Tsaa
Aguaruna <Peru>: Atsá
Aguateco <Guatemala>: Ci
Ariti <Brazil>: Maicá
Auca <Ecuador>: Ba
Auca: Wín
Aymara <Bolivia, Peru, and Chile>: Janiwa
Aymara: Janiw
Aymara: Jani
Aymara: Janixä

Boyubi <Bolivia>: Awíje

Cakchiquel <Guatemala>: Maan
Carib <Suriname, Venezuela, and Guyana>: Nonta
Charagua <Bolivia>: Ándi
Chiriguano <Bolivia>: Ani
Chontal <Guatemala>: Xani
Chontal: Ma
Chontal: Hañí
Chorti <Guatemala>: Ma
Chorti: Nian yahr
Chuj <Guatemala>: Ma

Gaviao <Brazil>: Áo
Gaviao: Óhv
Guaja <Brazil>: Nã'ã
Guarani <Argentina, Brazil, Bolivia, and Paraguay>: Nahániri
Guarani: Ahaniri

Hixkary <Brazil>: Hra
Huambisa <Peru>: Atsa

Ixil <Guatemala>: Ye'
Izonceno <Bolivia>: Ani

Jacaltec <Guatemala>: Mach
Jacaru < South America>: Isha

Kaipipende <Bolivia>: Áni
Kamayura <Brazil>: Anité
Kanjobal <Guatemala>: K'amaq
Kanjobal: C'am
Karawatarenda <Bolivia>: Áni
Kawesqar <Chile>: Kiép
Kayabi <Brazil>: Eém
Kekchi <Guatemala>: Ink'a'
Kekchi: Ma
Kuna <Panama>: Suli

Lagunillas <Bolivia>: Áni

Mam <Guatemala>: Mi
Mam: Min
Mapudungun <Chile>: Mü
Mayupampa <Bolivia>: Aepotáa
Miskito <Nicaragua and Honduras>: Apia
Mopamaya <Guatemala>: Ma'

Parana <Bolivia>: Aní
Parintintin <Brazil>: Nãhã

Paumari <Brazil>: Iniani
Paumari: Hari'a
Pauserna <Bolivia>: Áni
Pipil <El Salvador>: Inte
Pipil: Tee
Pipil: Tesu
Pocomam <Guatemala>: Ma
Pocomam: Ntaj
Pocomam: Ntax
Pocomam: Ta

Quechua <Andes of South America>: Ama
Quechua Ancashino <Peru>: Manam
Quechua Cochabambino <Bolivia>: Mana
Quechua Cuzqueno: <Bolivia>: Manan
Quiche <Guatemala>: Ma
Quiche: Mantaj
Quichua <Ecuador and Argentina>: Mana

Rapanui <Easter Island>: Ina
Redondo Tupi-Guarani <Ecuador>: Haeñum
Resigaro <Peru>: Nií
Resigaro: Niíkó
Resigaro: Niíkámí

Sacapultec <Guatemala>: Taj
Saramaccan <Suriname and French Guyana>: Ná
Saramaccan: Nõnö
Shipibo <Peru>: Icáma
Sranan <Suriname and Aruba>: Nono

Taki Taki <French Guyana>: Nono
Tehuelche <Argentina>: Gom
Tsafiqui <Ecuador>: Te
Tupi <Brazil>: Mbaa
Tupi: Naani
Tupi: Naanikwaw
Tupi: Naani mia

Urubu <Brazil>: Anin
Uspantec <Guatemala>: Ta'

Villamontes Tupi Guarani <Bolivia>: Awigi

Waura <Brazil>: A
Waura: Aitsa

Xerente <Brazil>: Anrê
Xeta <Brazil>: Ñiá

15

Colorful Commentary

From vitamin l there is a lot to gain. And all the time laughter will at least provide a temporary escape from the pain. Now sit back, relax, and let those lips speak with a smile.

The purpose of this section is to make fun of the inadequacies oftentimes present within the no-good man. Besides, everyone needs a good laugh now and then, and laughter serves a very vital and significant purpose. Laughter is therapy for the heart. The joy of life is truly contained in laughter. The heart cannot weep forever. Tears cannot forever flow down the cheeks of a woman's face. Besides, where does a woman go once her body has lost its ability to produce any more tears and has become dehydrated? What is the next step after drowning in sorrow?

In times of pain, the ability to recognize the humor in things can help initialize the healing process. This will allow one to release and replace some of that internal anger and frustration with a smile. It also reinforces the idea that everything is going to be all right. It helps one realize the situation is not that bad after all. In fact, things could be much worse. Even if only for a short time, the feeling that those couple of seconds can provide by taking the heart and mind adrift from the sea of sorrow is worth far more than what words can express.

After the laughter and the no are spoken at the no-good man, then no explanation is required. For a no-good man is never worthy of an explanation of his abandonment. Thus, if the no-good man has the audacity to want to know why the decision was made to dismiss him, give him some colorful commentary.

The following are not to be taken literally. I stress respect and therefore will always show respect.

If you were the last man on earth, I would learn how to be a lesbian.

This happens to be a question that roams through my mind all day. How, oh how, did you manage to escape from the ASPCA?

Could you please answer this question so that I may learn? Why does your breath + my hair = an instant perm?

Being that you are a natural pain in the ass, it seems to me that your mother should have named you Hemorrhoid.

On many occasions I have been told that the reason why you're really not that into me is because I have a hole and not a pole.

There's no wondering why you're such an ass. Being that you were born out of the back of your mother, you never had a chance to be anything else.

My first name is not sanitation and my last name is not department. So what does that mean? It means that all I deal with is class so that leaves someone else to take out the trash.

The only mate a stray dog deserves is a stray cat. Now all you have to do is take yourself back to the kennel and meow that!

You are not as cute as a poodle or as strong as a pit bull. You're definitely in a canine class all by yourself.

Being that you were conceived in a hotel during the holidays, there is no wonder why you're a male whore.

When you depart from this Earth, at least we'll finally find out if all dogs really do go to Heaven.

It is bewildering how you can still be floating around through life. I always thought that a piece of shit was supposed to be flushed down the toilet.

I should have known that you would not be into me like that when you told me how you love the Banana Republic but hate the Gap.

You know I often get you confused with a female. Well obviously, that's because you have no balls.

You're lucky they don't put your meat in a taco. Poor Taco Bell and that cute little dog would go out of business.

Rice-A-Roni. Now do I really have to explain the reason why you will never ever bone me?

I have always wondered why you love Big Macs so much. Nothing on you is big, but everything sure is whack. What you should be ordering is a Happy Meal. That comes in much smaller, unsatisfying portions, just like you.

Do not get mad at me. Mother Nature gave you that pussycat three inches above your knees.

It's a good thing you aren't a plane. Paid passengers and standbys would be stranded, but could you really blame the pilots for not wanting to go anywhere near your pitiful cockpit?

Since two times two is four, and I don't need you anymore, please do not hesitate to find your way to the door.

You have an abundance of chromosomes but a lack of testosterone. So I'm leaving you all alone and without a home.

When I first met you, I thought that you were a winner. But I'm sorry because I was mistaken. You are nothing but a low-budget chicken dinner. And you could never imagine how disappointed I was to find out that your meat wasn't even worth the money.

At first I was upset when you called me a cunt. But then I realized that you don't urinate standing up, so all is forgiven!

One, two, three, four, I don't want a fake man knocking on my door. Five, six, seven, eight, better hurry to the homeless shelter before it's too late.

I know a lot of inquiring minds always wanted to know what happened to Rosemary's baby from that movie. Aw, now look at you! You are all grown up.

I'm going to let you go so you can play tic-tac-toe with your ho. But make sure you play the O, because that's not only what you are, it also represents how much you're worth.

You're lucky they don't sell your meat in the supermarket because your Purdue just doesn't do it. That's right! No one can get full off of that.

You are a waste and disgrace to the human race. You are truly a pathetic piece of penis who needs to be on the CDC's disease list.

If I took you to an appraiser, they would actually charge me to tell me that you're worthless.

I need a man who's like orange juice with calcium added that's good for the bones. Not a man who's like Kool-Aid, cheap, bad for the skin, and a cavity on the soul.

Your first name should be Nick, middle name A, and last name Lodeon. Why? Because you were made for a girl, not a woman.

Jerk off! Now don't get excited, because what I really mean is leave me alone.

I am not a daycare center. I do not have time to babysit a boy. If you want to learn how to become a man, first buy a Boyz II Men album and learn how to increase the size of your ham.

Not even John wants your hand cock. So how in the world can you figure that I do?

It's a good thing you don't live on a farm. You and your entire family would be deprived of calcium. Because if you can't even milk me, then you know not a damn thing is coming out of a cow.

"Giddy up, horse!" were my words after two minutes. I guess you aren't a thoroughbred after all.

You know the sanitation department isn't doing their job. If they were, then you wouldn't be here.

It's not the size of the ship, it's the way you navigate the seas. And I must say you are no Christopher Columbus. But one thing is for sure, you have to start looking for the discovery of new land, because this territory is no longer yours.

When I first met you, I thought you had tuberculosis. But then after some time, I came to realize your face is just naturally atrocious.

There are a lot of doctors who are jealous of you. After all, they had to actually go to four years of medical school to get their MD when you had one all along: a miniature dick.

Incompetent is as a fool does. And somehow you manage to do both like the true professional that you are.

How dare you? Just because a toilet bowl could not accept all of your shit, you are trying to give me the remainder of it. What I suggest is that you try to find a toilet that is large enough to accept all of what you have to release because shit and me just don't have compatibility.

I used to visualize us having a child together. But now I have come to realize that this would not only be an insult to me, but it would be an embarrassment to my ovaries.

These are just some words of wisdom to the inexperienced. The next time you think about sitting in a restaurant to have your meal, you should take it to go. Why? Well, it's because you need to learn how to eat out.

You are truly a Homo sapien. Way more homo than sapien, though.

Your autobiography should be named *The Little Engine that Wished It Could but Never Ever Can!*

You could be a used car salesman. Why? Because not only did you lie about the efficiency and durability of your engine, but you also said you had low mileage. Unfortunately, both turned out to be false. After being driven for only one minute, I mean one mile, not only did you break down, but you needed a tune-up right after that. What a waste of machinery! From now on, I only stick to diesel engines.

Sticks and stones may break my bones but that little wiener of yours will never ever hurt me.

Has anyone ever told you that you should try to work for CBS? And no, it is not because of your potential to be a good journalist. It's because of your constant bullshit.

When we first got together, I thought you were gold. But it is difficult to tell the difference between gold, bronze, and shit because they all have similar coloring. And guess which one you are? If you don't know, then all that I can say is that you cannot win this at the Summer Olympics.

After majoring in foolology for four years, rather than graduating from an institution with a BA, you graduated with a BBS: that's a bachelor of bullshit. But hey, you did graduate with a 4.0, after all. That's right, summa cum laude all the way!

If your cock was stock, Wall Street would have to be relocated to Poor Street.

The real reason why I'm not into you is because you're a no-good man who isn't worth a damn.

Yeah, that's right! I called you an asshole. If the hole happens to fit, then jump into it. Besides, you jump into every other open hole out there. But it is the hole of an ass that so happens to be the perfect fit for you.

The only minute that I like comes in the form of a maid, and that's from oranges—Minute Maid. Therefore, you only have one minute before you self-destruct. Fifty-nine, fifty-eight…one, I'm sorry Mr. No-Good Minute Man, but your time is now up.

Although you have been dismissed, I can guarantee that you'll be back. Why am I so certain? Because just like a leprechaun, a no-good man will always find his way back to gold.

The sweeter the speech, the sourer the speaker. And with all the cavities in your mouth, you are the sole reason your dentist is still in business.

Your mother has to be a donkey, because only a donkey could give birth to a real jackass.

Out of all the baseball fields in the world, your small balls had to enter into mine. I'll tell you one thing and you can mark my word on it: Whatever field you are heading into next, I can guarantee you won't be hitting any home runs with those things.

When you first took out your pen to expose your ink, I finally realized that you are indeed the weakest link.

I would say fuck you, but who in their right mind would do that?

Why do fools fall in love? I have no idea. Ask your parents to find out that one because only two fools can create a retard.

Your nickname should be Charmin. And this is not because you have charm, but because you are only good for one brief use, wiping an ass, and then getting flushed down the toilet.

Would you like to know the real reason why I'm leaving you? Well it's because I am tired of changing diapers. And then you think you have really made an improvement because now you wear pull-ups. When you can be a man and finally fit into some briefs, literally, like Hanes His Way, then I will continue to do things my way.

Now I understand why you love playing football so much. If I were a man and had no balls, I would love to play with a big one every chance that I had.

I've always wondered what two dog breed mixes you are. And I have come to the conclusion that it must be half bulldog and half shih tzu. Obviously, that's why you've learned how to perfect the art of bullshitting.

Do not, I repeat, do not be mad at me because you're disguised as a rooster but really a hen that produces estrogen.

In order to be my man you must first be a man and not a boy with a one-inch ham.

I am here contemplating two words that can summarize the height of your sexual excitement. The only thing that comes to mind is, "thumbs up!"

If I had to choose a dog breed to describe you, I would have to say the cock less, I mean cocker spaniel. I truly do apologize for the mistake.

I hope you don't think that I hate you. But if you do, that happens to be false. I just hate the air you breathe that allows you to sustain life.

I hope you don't think that I hate you. But if you do, that happens to be false. I just hate the ovary and sperm that produced you.

When you first revealed what lies between your thighs, I was shocked. I believe my first words were, "Who are you planning to hurt with that?" You can't hurt a groundhog, let alone a human with your one-inch barrel. Now could you please redeliver that back to the underground tunnel you got it from, and don't let it back out until February, or how about April 1? That's your day, the day of the fool!

You're lucky that you weren't an American Revolutionary soldier and a traitor. If that were the case, your name would have been Benedick-less Arnold.

You know, I should have known you were a dog from the first time we met. Instead of you shaking my hand, you tried to lick me. Then you lifted up your hind leg to take a leak. What more signs could I possibly have needed?

I often wonder why you act so cocky. I guess a man with a little penis needs to compensate somehow.

Please do not taint my diamond eyes with your cubic zirconium lies. So would you please do me and yourself a favor by taking that cheap shit back to the pawnshop where you got it from?

If you were a Boeing 747, you would be destined for location nowhere. Why? Because your broken wing can't take anyone anywhere. But if you could practice durability, the Concorde would have *nothing* on you because you would certainly be able to reach the intended destination in approximately one minute. And I believe that is record-breaking time.

I can guarantee that every woman would agree there should be a no-good man maxi pad with wings. Once his use is completed, if he doesn't fly away on his own, then he could be properly discarded.

I can understand that you are a dog, but at least your mother could have trained you to go on the paper before she brought you to the kennel.

"Roof, Roof," was the sound I heard from my dog's mouth. Since you speak dog, and that's obvious because you are one, could you please translate that into English for me? Thank you!

I really feel for your mom. Her real-life testimony should be in the *Guinness Book of World Records*. Why? Because I know that it is an ordeal to have a human baby living inside of your womb, but to have a puppy living inside a human's uterus is truly an amazing medical phenomenon.

I can recall the day I first saw Junior. It happened to be on April Fool's Day. My first words were, "Boy, that's a really cruel joke. Now where's the real one?"

They should make playing cards that represent the individuals playing them. In your case, Ace would have to be changed to Ass.

You really do have things misconstrued. You have obviously missed the fact that we do not live in a Socialist society. Your penis is private, not public property for the good of the whole community.

When you dropped your pants, I could have sworn that you pawned in your penis for a pussycat. Then when I went to pet it, it meowed. "What the hell is going on here?" was my response.

I should have known you would have not been able to handle the class and sophistication of a luxury vehicle. It's probably because you have been driving Pintos all your life.

I really do advise you to adopt a cat because from now on, that's the only pussy you're getting!

Please, AT&T does not live here anymore. Not only has your phone service been disconnected, but you will not be reaching out and touching me anymore. Now how do you like those touch-tone apples?

When you first pulled down your pants I said, "Call 911, I want to report a robbery." But when you told me that I just needed to have a magnifying glass handy, I advised you that most universities have a research center for people with conditions like yours. "If I can't see it with my eyes, then I am truly petrified," were my final words.

Have you ever realized that you, as well as many other no-good men, are reborn on a daily basis? But only this birth doesn't take place in a hospital bed. It takes place in a bathroom. "Oh shit, that's right, oh Sugar Honey Iced Tea!"

I can remember when you told me on one hot summer's day how you felt like shit. I believe my response was, "You know, it is truly a blessing when you can finally feel the way you look."

Yes! I did it to myself. I should have listened to that saying, "Lie down with a dog and get up with fleas." Now in addition to my doctor's bills, I have vet bills. Lord, have mercy!

Before you purchase a house, I think you will find that a con-dom-mini-mum is much more suitable for you.

Your mouth should come with a lifetime supply of toilet paper because of all the shit that comes out of it.

Are you really surprised that after being examined by your doctor he recommended you take vitamin D? It just goes to show that it's not only me who believes that you have a little wee-wee.

You can take vitamins A, B, C, and D, but nothing can compare to vitamin me. And without it, wherever you stand, you will forever be a malnourished man.

So now that you've been dismissed, you want to have insults? Well if you really want to make me laugh, just pull down your pants. One word, hysterical! So hush, little puppy, and put yourself to use by fetching my slippers.

16

Steps
2
Success:
The Proper Way
2
Heal

To breathe a sigh of fresh air. To rid the pollution that plagues and dilutes the atmosphere. To finally be free is to inhale that new fresh air and release that which is toxic. Now breathe in. Take a moment. And now breathe out. For a new day awaits.

Once a woman has amputated the infectious no-good man from her existence, then she can begin the healing process toward prosperity and growth. Learning how to embrace individual change is important in this transitional period. Unfortunately, some may not seek to alter their situation for fear of readjustment or having to change an accustomed and familiar pattern that provides security.

Commonly, people reject change because they fear the foreign. Unlike change, it is convenient and easy. This familiarity allows for people to feel secure with how they handle situations and continue on in those ways. This occurs because the mind is so conditioned to thinking in a certain way and toward a certain goal. Therefore, the ability to embrace anything else or even think about pursuing something outside of that comfort zone does not incorporate itself into the thinking process, especially when the goal is, "how to keep my no-good man satisfied and happy" rather than, "how can I go about strengthening myself and my future." This enables an individual to continue on in their set ways, neglecting positive change.

My dear woman, you must not fear change. You must not fear embracing the unfamiliar and changing for the positive. Embracing just one step will allow you to move at least one inch forward on a path toward individual redemption and make an enriching difference and improvement in your life.

Write the Goal(s) Down: The very first step toward success after acknowledging the problem is to write down the goal or goals. This acts as a constant reminder to the mind and body and gives them something to focus on. Place the paper in a location that is in plain view. I also encourage a woman to write down any negative comments that were said or save any hurtful notes that the no-good man sent. This will be a good form of motivation to move on.

Allow for the Heart to Heal: Give the body ample time to emotionally recuperate before entering into another relationship. How much time is ample? This is defined by the individual. Some women take longer to emotionally heal than others. This is the best option to heal a heart, which should also include abstinence. This means no penetration or oral gratification. This might be difficult for some who are accustomed to having a steady supply of sexual satisfaction. So what happens when there is an itch? As with any itch, a woman can scratch it herself. Besides, fingers can always use the exercise. That's right! "Getting to know yourself" can be given a new and innovative meaning. There is a great advantage to self-exploration. A woman will always be able to account for the where-abouts of her hand.

Do Not Fear Solitude: Never fear being single. A woman must realize that moving on does not require another man to be waiting there to finish off what the last man did not. Embrace this time alone. This will actually allow a woman time to learn about her true self, including how much strength she has. I encourage a woman to become reacquainted with her current definition of self and compare this to what she has always desired to be.

Remove the Victim Mentality: Rid that weak part which believes self did not play a role in the abuse. Instead, implement a victorious and strong mentality. "If you are not a part of the solution, then you are a part of the problem." We must learn how to take responsibility for our actions or inactions. There comes a time when a woman needs to cease blaming the no-good man for the situation and begin blaming herself for being an accomplice. There is allowance given to the abuser from the abused to treat them in that manner. Remember that a man will only treat a woman the way a woman allows him to. There is always the choice of leaving the relationship. The reason why he prospers and the woman declines is because the woman chooses not to leave. When this fact is accepted, it is possible for a woman to think of herself as a courageous survivor who is fully in charge of what happens in her life. The body will then act upon this belief. A victim walks around with a feeling of pity, a feeling of defeat, and a lack of a warrior's spirit. A victim has already accepted her loss and therefore is most likely to have a sullen outlook upon the life that lies ahead. This will then make a woman complacent, leading her to the next no-good man.

Do Not Seek Revenge: Stay away from the man who is responsible for those tangled emotions. This will only make a woman seem weak and dependent upon that person for happiness. Nothing will make that man hurt more than seeing his former lover move on and live life to the fullest without contacting him.

Learn How to Distinguish between Want Versus Need: A woman may want a man but a woman does not need a man. The only things a human being needs are what are imperative to survival. This includes oxygen, food, as well as a stable job to provide money to buy necessities. Everything else is for pleasure. The only time that a woman should be involved with a man is when there is stability.

Resolve Any Open Wounds: Any emotional baggage should be worked on in order to progress. This applies to anyone with whom there may be some friction or a grudge. This will free up the heart and allow for progress. Loved ones should be kept in contact with. Resolving these open wounds will prevent the possibility of future manipulation. If there is a need, seek counseling or other professional help. Moving on with life and progressing should be the number-one goal. Putting an end to unresolved issues will help a woman see herself and her life in a new and improved light.

Release Any Frustration, Pain, or Anger: Yell! Do whatever comes naturally. All of this will help get rid of those negative feelings. A woman should then revise her outlook and be grateful for what she has, rather than being disappointed for what she lacks. Realize that many people look down from their positions in a higher and more spiritual place, wishing they could be granted the ability to live another day. Besides, life affords us the ability to undo any anger and change this by channeling all of that energy into a more positive pastime.

Avoid All Dependencies: Dependencies on sex, food, alcohol, drugs, clothes, or any other item of materialism do not strengthen the body. They make the body depend on these things for gratification. There is always exercise, Tai Chi, and meditation. This will revive a woman's mental and physical well-being. A woman may even wish to travel in order to experience new horizons or environments which will take her mind away from issues that plague her. A woman may wish to read a good book. Explore information or education. Sing, write, or act. These are the options that I encourage a woman who is having difficulty moving on to do.

Vocalize Emotions: A woman should express her pain to others, especially those who have walked in her shoes. Ask them how they coped and recuperated from the heartache. I encourage a woman to take the time out to not only hear, but listen and absorb the information they share. She should associate herself with people who can inspire and encourage her toward progress. This will help her along in the healing process. Knowing that you are not alone will give the body a boost of energy to fight and win. Turning to friends, family, a psychologist, or a support group to assist with emotional healing is also a positive step. However, if no one wants to listen or there is difficulty in expressing personal feelings, then a piece of paper always has open ears and patience for a pen. Keep a diary. One of the advantages writing offers is that a piece of paper will never complain or find fault. It will never be judgmental or critical. There is no danger of gossip, so a woman can feel comfortable about expressing her feelings.

Have Confidence: A lack of self-confidence and determination keeps a person from achieving their goals. This is responsible for the body's inability to achieve. It can also destroy any desire to do so. A woman must always believe she possesses the ability to achieve any personal goal. Victory will be her reward.

Discover Spirituality and Religion: Spirituality will open up the heart and soul, making it easier to forgive. Finding spirituality increases strength, tranquility, and internal harmony. This allows a woman to have a new and improved outlook upon life. The baggage of bitterness and pain will be removed. When we continue to work on all the things that plague our ability to be peaceful, then we will find happiness.

Allow Forgiveness into the Heart: Everyone is worthy of forgiveness, even if they do not make an attempt to ask for it. This is not done to console their conscience, but to console the person who forgives. The baggage that tangled emotions bring to someone's life prevents that individual from experiencing the ultimate gift of prosperity and growth. A woman must never allow bitterness to consume her heart and life. A woman must learn to live and let live.

Cut Off All Interaction with the Man in Question: There should be no excuses to stay in touch with the no-good man, unless there is a child at stake. Even if there was an established relationship with his family, there still should be no contact with them. There should be no association with anyone or anything that is going to make that attachment remain. A woman must try her best not to reminisce upon the "good times." Cut up, shred, or throw away any gifts from him. Let the past stay in the past and only worry about what stands in the present and lies in the future. Keeping items that have a connection to him will maintain that emotional attachment to him.

Be Active, Not Passive: A woman should be assertive, directly confronting any problem. Be open and honest about what bothers and hurts the body. Do not run away from it.

Practice Unconditional Self-Love: A woman must look into the mirror and love the reflection she sees. Whatever imperfections exist, she should still embrace and love them. A woman must realize that she was created in the image that God envisioned, and God does not make crap. Everything a woman has is for a reason. She should also learn how to accept the fact that everything she possesses helps in her definition of self.

Discover and Embrace Individuality: If a woman has yet to completely and accurately define who she is, she should take time out to really contemplate her future, passions, and interests. If there is difficulty in determining this, then exploring numerology and astrology can assist in an objective analysis of where potential weaknesses and strengths lie. I encourage a woman to list her positive qualities or strengths, as well as her negative qualities or weaknesses on two separate sheets of paper. Focus on the positives. Try to improve the weaknesses and negative qualities. If a woman is unable to eliminate her negative qualities, then she should try to focus all of her negative energy into something positive. This will inspire a woman to find out what defines herself and what she has to offer. This will allow her to know she is worthy and deserving of someone who will recognize and acknowledge the internally and externally beautiful person she is, as well as the positive qualities that she can bring to a relationship. Doing this reinforces the fact that, "I am somebody."

Questions:

Can the Former No-Good Man Be a Friend? A woman must consider the following and answer truthfully. Is there faith that this man will be a true and genuine friend? A true friend is someone who a woman can run to when there is emotional hurt and the need to vent about the no-good man. A friend is genuine and dependable through good times and bad. The no-good man has already let the woman down and proven himself to be uncaring and inconsiderate in a romantic relationship. Who is to say that he will have a change of heart and display compassion and dedication to a woman as a friend? There is no certain way to indicate that he will or will not, but a woman should consider the evidence from the past and let it guide her to the right decision in the present. The last thing a person needs is a no-good friend.

Will I look upon him in a monogamous way or do I only seek to keep my options open for future relations? This is an important question. A woman must realize that friendship does not include sex. Sex can complicate a friendship. Sex can destroy a friendship. If sex is what a woman seeks, then the no-good man is not the one who should fill that void. He has proven himself unworthy of what the woman has to offer. I would also advise a woman that keeping this man as a friend will only delay resolving her tangled emotions.

Does the No-good Man Deserve a Second Chance at Love? Is everyone really deserving of a second chance? Sometimes a person can act so outrageously that it deems them unworthy of a second chance. I encourage a woman to explore the possibility that what happened before could happen again. A woman must consider how severe he messed up the first time. The fact that he messed up in the first place should be motivation enough not to give him a chance to do it again. Can the heart endure that pain and devastation twice?

Will there be trust? Does a woman really wish to restart the healing process from the beginning if this turns out to be a horrible mistake?

To think about giving a second chance is to still be in love. This may also indicate that the healing process was never adequately initiated, let alone nurtured. In order to give anyone a second chance, that person must have to *show and prove* they have made a change for the better. And the mere statement, "I've changed" does not cut it. This man has to demonstrate this first, where the woman can properly evaluate his actions and see if they are different or similar to his past behavior. This way a woman can evaluate if the change is legitimate, genuine, and sincere. I would also recommend a waiting period before deciding to make any definite decisions.

Unfortunately, I cannot answer this question. A woman is going to have to dig deep down into her soul and think with her head to find the answer. However, what I will warn is that you reap what you sow. We should not wish to experience so much negativity that life is spent trying to mend the mistakes of the past. In other words, a woman should make sure not to be a victim for the second, third, or fourth time around.

17

Excerpts
of
Encouragement

A woman should let her tears be small drops of liquid bullets that do not symbolize defeat, but will provide ammunition for perseverance, endurance, and strength to battle life's challenges. This will come to reveal the true meaning of the word overcome.

The process of healing and gaining a positive outlook is sometimes very difficult. Although the Devil's temptations may seek to steer us off of the path toward individual progress and happiness, we must always keep our eyes on the prize because the good that God has in store is more worthy and worthwhile than anything evil can tempt us with. The journey may be rough and it may seem very hard to reach the top of that mountain where the air is so much cleaner than below, but lo and behold, the goal is much closer than we expect. We must not give up and keep our heads arched up because when the going gets rough, we just gotta get tough.

The following represents some inspirational excerpts that will help conquer the battle of moving on and being victorious in the war against negativity. So keep that head arched to the sky. It is because you are a woman and that happens to be the most important reason why.

-1-

Although strong women may finish last in love, we always finish first in life. And that's because we never cease to fight for what's right. When others consider it wrong, we stand strong, on firm ground because we do not tolerate being mistaken as fools and stick around. Believe in yourself always because at the end of the night, you may be the only one around to console yourself in life.

-2-

The sky is not the limit because beyond the sky there are galaxies. The only limit that restricts one's ability to reach for the stars in this life is death. Realize the potency of your potential and know that the only two things that cannot be achieved in this lifetime are no thing and nothing.

-3-

I am beautiful inside and out. And this is a fact that is without a doubt. A man can never make me succumb, for I am number one. I do not need a man to succeed. The only person that I need begins with an M and ends with an E. And until I realize this, I will never be free.

-4-

A woman should always carry herself with pride and hold her head up high. For a woman is a queen and does not need a man to justify her worth. A woman was not recently created this way, she was royalty from birth. A woman was placed on this Earth to worship and never be disobeyed by a mate because her fate will not tolerate such a disgrace. And with all this information, a woman must always place herself first. So then one must ask, if a real woman is all of this with a dash of class, then how can she possibly tolerate a man who treats her like trash?

-5-

In life, some rain must fall. But regardless of the storm, you can weather it all. The thing that separates the winners from the losers is their undying will to survive. And that is the same type of fire that will never die. Courage that leads to victory is the name of the winner's game. Weakness that leads to defeat is how the loser remains the same. Never to move forward in life because to them it is not worth the fight. The loser will always search for less and never more. If you are so afraid to confront the battle, then how can you expect to win the war?

-6-

Some of us die to live and some of us live to die. Some of us cannot go through life without a man by our side. A woman is not a woman because a man makes her to be. And a woman is not a woman because she has two children at twenty-three. And a man is not a man because his penis can rise high. Shit, half of the time a man does not even respect what lies in between some thighs. Womanhood is received when a girl has become divine. Manhood is deemed when a boy's manhood he can define. Respect is given when respect is earned. Those who breathe life into this meaning have already earned theirs, and if you have not yet to do so, then now it's your turn.

-7-

Do not cry if you bleed. Patch your wound up, let it heal, and go right back out there and succeed. Crying is meant for children and cry they will do. But if you are an adult and still crying, then I have no sympathy for you. Within a tear is fear, and within the ability to fight is might. I'm not saying you cannot show emotion, but when you begin to act upon your beliefs, you'll show yourself a whole lot more devotion. But what becomes of the meaning of devotion when it is directed in the opposite motion and once the no-good man acts up he is still granted some of that powerful love potion? I know it's hard, and I know it's rough, but sometimes, just believing that you can do it will be more than enough. And although I must, but really do hate to admit that, yes, feelings are a part of the equation confined within life's big plan. But still a woman should never let them conquer her ability to stand up to a no-good man.

-8-

I may not dress in army fatigues but I am a soldier nonetheless. So do not even think for one minute that your harmful bullets and evil ways can penetrate through my vest. Now I live by the term "survival of the fittest." So therefore being a weak woman is not permitted. With strength now incorporated into my vocabulary and applied on a daily basis, I have the determination and will to face it, meaning all of the obstacles that confront me on my way toward elevation. With this manifest destiny securely intact, I will now cut the bonds that signified our relationship with my newly purchased knife. And with that said, I dismiss you, no-good man, now and forever out of the dictionary that defines the meaning of my life.

-9-

Pollution does not only exist in the air; it also exists in the soul. The hearts of many are plagued with bitterness and prone to be so cold. Colder than the winter days of December, so heartbroken that the summer days of warmth, they cannot remember. Just hold onto faith, and let the blood that flows through your veins also touch your heart. Thus, you will be rewarded with the ultimate gift. Those deeply engraved feelings of hatred will magically depart.

-10-

At the end of the tunnel, there is always a light filled with so much insight. When you reach it, do not put on shades to protect your eyes from the ultraviolet rays. The truth should never be avoided. Regardless of the lies that try to bring forth that black night, day-light will always come to reveal a truth that shines bright.

Inspiration through Poetry

The Equation of a Real Woman's Worth
$.10? $1.00? $100? $1,000? The Answer = No x 4. Vagina + Ovaries + Two X Chromosomes + Breasts + Menstrual Cycle + PMS + Lactate + Childbirth + Lips + Hips + Ass + Sass + Class + Sincerity + Respect + Grace + Pride + Poise + Honesty + Dedication + Integrity + Compassion + Independence + Intelligence + Fortitude+ Being So Damn Divine and Fine = No Less Than an Infinite Amount x 29.

Platinum Pussycat
When the vagina comes too easy, she's labeled as a slut. Then when it takes too long to open up, she's considered difficult and too much.
If you were to ask me which one do I choose, I would have to say the latter. In my world of rules and relationships, it takes more than

a fine face to make my crossed legs unravel. With me, it's the mind and intellect that truly matter.

For what lies three feet below my face and deep within the depths of my waist is equivalent to what's found inside the mines of Africa. It is not silver or bronze, and it is not even gold. It is a diamond dipped in platinum, and when it's finally revealed, oh what a sight to behold. Meow!

Jacob the Jeweler

Jacob the Jeweler does not have anything on me. For the waiting list to gain access to my jewels runs more than ten months deep. Subject to background checks and an intense investigation. Why, you ask? Because all of this is necessary before penetration.

You see a woman cannot just let any Harry, Tom, or Dick enter into the tomb of her womb. Who knows? He could be a grave digger disguised as Robin Hood, ready to steal from her riches and also be the same exact man who refers to all women as bitches.

A woman must realize that when she allows for a grave digger to run off with the jewels inside of her tomb, meaning heart, vagina, and trust, she has allowed for her body to be disgraced in the name of lust. Only to discover that not only did this thief make off with a precious gem that he could neither afford nor deserve, but this man who claimed to have her best interest at heart was never really her man, confidante nor friend, but only her lover waiting to get his hands on one thing, then depart to another.

So please, my dear woman, do not allow for sex to be sold in the name of your soul. Instead just let that no-good man be a fool for your gold.

STRENGTH

Strength is me, and strength is who I am. Weakness I will battle, and strength is where I will stand. I am strength fortified. I am strength multiplied. I am strength never denied.

Even if I have no weapons, strength will still allow me to fight. Strength will padlock my pussy and say, "You ain't getting none tonight." Strength will force me to stand up for myself, allowing me to take action when enough is enough. This strength will also be my force, allowing me to move forward when the storm gets rough.

This strength in me is like the Atlantic Ocean, filled with so much life to sea and giving me energy like a potion. This strength in me runs so damn deep. But please do not ever mistake it for running six feet underneath. You see, this strength in me will never be rest in peace. It is engraved in my heart and neither negative words nor put-downs will ever make it depart.

It is because of this strength that I now have **S**uccess. It is because of this strength that my fears have been put to the **T**est. It is because of this strength that I am **R**eady to conquer. It is because of this strength that I can **E**ndure above and beyond in life. It is because of this strength that I will **N**ever relinquish my might.

It is because of this strength that I now look in the mirror and see **G**old. It is because of this strength that even though I am only five feet, I will still stand **T**all. And it is because of this strength that my body is now w**H**ole.

For doing all of this, I would like to say thank-you to strength for allowing me to see. Thank-you, strength, for setting me free. But most importantly, I would like to thank strength for believing in me.

18

Dating Guidelines

Once those breaths have been taken and that clean air makes its way into the system, we must keep it, hold onto it, and try our best to never allow for pollution to enter us once again.

The ultimate purpose of this book is to not only advise the reader of the ways of the no-good man but to also provide preventative measures to deter future relations with the no-good man. Controlling fate is impossible, so even if crossing paths with the no-good man is inevitable, the most important thing is being able to say no once his status is determined. Once we can say no to the no-good man and yes to ourselves, we can focus on finding a good man and discovering 999 ways to say yes to him.

In order to prevent this mistake again, there has to be an application of certain principles and relationship guidelines. Regardless of how fine he is, they must still be followed. The ultimate test is not in one's ability to build up enough courage to say no, but to do the very best in not becoming a victim to the no-good man's game once again. It is true that everyone has flaws, but the objective at hand should ultimately be to find a man with the least amount of them.

Define What Love Means and What It is Supposed to Include: Learn how to distinguish between positive and negative love. Positive love promotes positive results and individual growth. Negative love diminishes a person's potential and overall mental, physical, and emotional state. As a result, now knowing and recognizing these two types of loves will help in the disposal of negative love.

Increase Individual Standards: Have high expectations. Remove *settle* from your vocabulary. Apply energy to defy obstacles. The application of this concept is valid in both life and relationships. When a woman fails to set the bar high enough for herself, this can open up the gateway to abuse and acceptance of nonsense. If a woman is bringing her A game, then there is no reason why she should accept someone who is only willing to give her a D level effort.

Learn How to Separate the Heart from the Head: These are two separate entities. One thinks and the other feels. In matters of negative love, we have to think with the head and not with the heart. Intelligence, not love, must make the decision on the basis of the man's action. If there is more negative than positive results from the relationship, then it is best left alone.

Develop a Manuscript: During the development of this book, I had to create a "no-good" manuscript. It is a good idea to develop a "good" manuscript when searching for a partner. A woman should think about her definition of a good man. Contemplate the most important standards. These are to be written in stone. Education, ethics, religion, and stability are all important factors. A woman should also consider the standards that she is willing to compromise on. Standards of a materialistic nature fall under this category. Remember that materialism does not define a good man. The heart, soul, and spirit do. After these questions are answered, a woman must adhere to this manuscript. A woman should not abandon it for the physical or the sexual. Never neglect substance for the superficial.

Develop a Businesswoman Mentality: Do not invest time, money, the heart, or any other valuable asset into anyone who has no potential or is not expected to yield a higher profit than the investment. As a general rule, if the benefit does not at least equal the investment, then you are wasting your time. Remember, the only thing that a cubic zirconium and a diamond have in common are the letters M, O, N and I, so say good-bye!

Adopt a No Tolerance Policy: Eliminate your ability to accept excuses and place the no-good man on the endangered species list. As soon as a man sees tolerance, he will continue with negative behavior. It should be one strike, a new baseball team.

Collect on Collateral: A woman should not do anything without a ring. Now *anything* may have a different meaning to each woman. Nonetheless, anything means to avoid a permanent relationship with the man before the initiation of complete commitment. Make him commit his life and finances to you. A woman has the right to secure her future interests. For espousal support + child support = more than just child support alone. Now keep in mind, the real collateral is in the vows. The ring just equals a promise to one day be able to collect. The vows equal the right to collect.

Adopt a Waiting Period Before Intimacy: There should be no oral sensation or penetration, for intimacy prepares the heart for love. However, if abstinence is out of the question, then shield the sausage. As tempting as raw meat may be, it is still no-good when consumed without thorough preparation. If a woman insists on riding a horse, then let it be Trojan style! A woman may also wish to have a waiting period before committing. The length of the waiting period is defined individually and should end when the woman feels as though there is nothing she could not answer about him just in case *America's Most Wanted* requests an interview. The waiting period before intimacy can be an effective way to decrease the chance of emotional attachment. Therefore, if this man does turn out to be no-good, then there will be less heartache.

Investigation Before Penetration: Investigation before penetration = a more pleasurable sensation. The time during the waiting period serves a special purpose and should be used effectively. If there is any confusion, then just repeat the alphabet, and you will see that "I" always comes before "P." Get to know the person that the penis is attached to rather than just the penis itself. Discover his personality prior to discovering his penis because the individual lies above the waist, not below it. Discover his likes, dislikes, goals, and future plans. Observe his body language and how he acts in public. Listen to what he says. It is quite surprising how many people cannot keep their stories straight. Be observant of how he treats others, specifically women and children. Ask: Why are you single in the first place? STD status is very important. What do you look for in a woman? Avoid naivety, but an open mind is good to have. After all, everyone deserves the benefit of the doubt. However, a woman should not just give her trust away. Remember, trust is earned after a person proves themselves by way of action. Thus, after every period, place a question mark, because a lot of what a person may claim to be could be very far from reality. Also, family and friends will often eventually volunteer information. A woman might be surprised at what some friends and family members have to say about him. Consider all of this information. Also, there is nothing wrong with having a background check done. This will reveal any skeletons trapped inside of the closet. As a result, a woman's decision of whether to proceed or not can be based on truthful information. Always remember that a secondary source will not always have an interest to protect.

Evaluate Priorities: If a woman is not at the top of her list, then she must ask herself why. A woman must place herself first, not second and surely not last. Yes, it is acceptable to place certain individuals on or above your level. But remember, *I* is capitalized for a reason. This does not only apply to the rule of writing but it is also applicable to the value of life. It demonstrates the significance of self. A woman must make the well-being of her heart, mind, and body her first priority before and after entering into a relationship with another. Once a man proves himself to be trustworthy and good by treating her with respect, then a woman can place him on the same level as herself. However, any man who is not willing to accept her decision or is not willing to place her as a top priority within his life should not be taken seriously.

Live Respectfully: Define respect, then apply this definition to self. Accept the fact that the body is a temple. This should motivate the mind to think twice before allowing just anyone to trespass and gain access to its hidden treasures. A woman must respect herself before she will be respected by others. When a woman has fully accepted the meaning of respect into her life, then she must not allow for anyone to treat her in a manner that is less than the definition. And a woman must always remember that a gentleman is attracted to a lady. If a woman carries herself like a stray cat, then she is destined to attract a stray dog.

19

Affirmation

Beauty is me. Beauty is you. But most importantly, real beauty is the image of those living diamonds who represent true womanhood.

My dear woman, always remember that you have to think with your head first and not with your heart or you are doomed for failure from the start. After the crying is over, there needs to be action. Take your time to sulk, but turn pain into profit by embracing the lesson that pain is trying to show you. Once your speech reflects your new way of thinking, do not only speak to preach but practice what you speak.

Repeat this affirmation when weakness begins to creep in:

I am beautiful. I love who I am. I cherish my body. I will do anything to protect my body. I refuse to let anyone abuse my body. I am worth being loved. I am first in my life. I refuse to place anyone before my well-being. I will never abandon my body. I will never abandon the love that I have for myself. I will never settle for less than the best. I will never allow someone else to think for me. I will always think for myself and utilize the power within my mind to answer the questions that I have. I will think with my head first and always.

I will say no to anyone who tries to diminish my worth. I will say no to anyone who seeks to promote negative growth within

me. I will say no to anyone who tries to hurt me physically, emotionally, or mentally. I will say no to a no-good man. I will say no to bitterness that tries to eat away and pollute my heart. I will say no to bitterness against myself and others who try to bring me down to their level of agony and misery. I will say no to anger that eats away at my ability to be happy.

I will say yes to internal salvation. I will say yes to strength wherever it may lie, whether it be underneath the darkest and dreariest locations or above the highest of mountains. I will say yes to anything that uplifts me and no to anything that tries to destroy me. I will say yes to forgiveness in order to allow pain and emotional scars to heal. I will say yes to my passions and desires that help me in a positive way. I will say yes to my potential and never seek to abandon it. I will say yes to using my potential. I will say yes to education and never cease learning.

I will always try to see the positive in all situations, no matter how negative they may be. I will release my burdens and sorrows and realize that I was given a life and am able to breathe and wake up every morning for a reason. I will take advantage of the opportunity that life has awarded me. I will always learn from my mistakes and experiences in life. I will always believe in who I am. I will always motivate, encourage, and inspire myself, even when others do not do the same. I will live my life for myself. I will never cease to improve who I am and strive to become a better person. I will never let anyone discourage me from my dreams. I will never allow for anyone to turn my dreams into nightmares.

I will say yes to my womanhood. For I am a strong woman, and I will never let myself or another forget that.

Best of wishes. You hold an esteemed and distinguished title: woman. And now is the opportunity to do that title proud and be the best woman you can possibly be. No one knows what life will hold, but never fear embarking on the journey. And always remember, there is only one obstacle that stands between you and victory: *you*.

Author Biography

Born on September 14, 1982, Mercedes A. Terzol was raised by her aunt, Augusta Terzol, and her grandmother, Dorothy Terzol. In the fall of 2000, she embarked upon an educational journey where she soon found herself majoring in political science; this would ignite her love for research and analysis. She has a passion for writing, which she describes as a "soul-searching experience that involves inner reflection." Numerology is her tool for spiritual guidance, giving her the ability to put personal experiences into perspective. "I can and I will" is Mercedes A. Terzol's outlook on goals yet to be conquered.

978-0-595-36760-3
0-595-36760-7